MY JOURNEY
TO THE
OTHER SIDE

BOOK 1

A Spiritual Memoir by Dee Delaney

Wrate's Publishing

My Journey to the Other Side (*The Truth is Within*, Book 1)

Published in 2023 by Wrate's Publishing

ISBN 978-1-7393758-2-9

Copyright © Dee Delaney, 2023, 2018

Edited and typeset by Wrate's Editing Services
www.wrateseditingservices.co.uk

This is a second edition. The first edition was published in 2018
by Garnet Press.

To my stars
Millie & Fionn

Contents

Prologue

Living from the heart

When we live from the heart, we live from a place of truth and honesty; where we do not judge ourselves or others. To do this we have to liberate our minds from the shackles of rigid beliefs systems that tell us we can and cannot behave in a certain way. As we free our minds we slowly start to transform our lives, one breath at a time. We begin to cultivate compassion for ourselves and others as we accept what is, understanding that the mirror of our own self is always showing us exactly where we are and what we need to purify. Nothing more, nothing less . Our job is to keep the faith and trust in life. As we connect to our consciousness it brings us back to our true nature - which is love As this connection deepens inside our hearts, we start to feel more alive. This brings peace to our lives, even in the most challenging of times. If we keep our hearts open, and allow the pure light of love that is within us all, to flow through our lives, without resistance, then we can and will create peace on earth.

This is what living from the heart means to me, and this is what I am focused on being. I am a woman of the world and I am living in my power raising my children while travelling the world and writing my stories. Each day I put one foot in front of the other and accept what life brings to me with an open heart. I am at peace with my life and my story.

But it wasn't always like this.

My journey has been long and hard and filled with endless loss as I spent years searching outside myself for happiness. By the age of 41, I had everything – or so I believed. I was living the Western dream that I thought everyone wanted. My life was consumed with doing. I had the job, the house, the children, the husband and the money. I was a woman driven by ambition and achievement, who struggled to get it all, and who worked damn hard to keep it. But in what I thought was a cruel twist of fate, just when I thought I had it all, the ground beneath me opened up and the life I knew and loved ended. I thought I'd lost everything, but actually, it was just the beginning.

This is my story, but it is also a universal story of love and loss. It is a story that I hope will give you, the reader, the strength to believe that love is stronger than death and has the power to heal the darkest wounds and the deepest despair. Through my story, I share a pathway to healing the self. It's for those who want to live in peace, and for those who want to learn how to be. It is a pathway without guilt, shame or regret. It is a path to love.

And so, it begins......

Part 1

One Woman's Story

Chapter 1

Cracking Open

❖

"In this story of one woman is the story of every woman. May you find the pathway into the spirit by which it was written."[1]

My journey back to mySelf started the day my beloved husband Tony died of a heart attack on Saturday 26th June 2010, while doing a charity walk in Scotland. Suddenly life as I knew it stopped and everything came into question.

You see, on paper, I was pretty much living the dream. I met my husband in 2002 on a blind date, and I knew instantly that I had met 'the one'. Our stories were so similar. We were from Irish backgrounds, in our mid-thirties, and we both had failed relationships that had produced a child each. Tony had a son called Nicholas, who was 14 when we met, and I had my daughter Millie, who was four. There were no buts with Tony, it was easy, and I suddenly had this love that made me feel complete. We married on 26th August 2004 in an extravagant wedding in Ireland and settled into the middle-class suburban dream in St Albans, England, a desirable commuter town just outside London. It was somewhere I had dreamed of living since I was a little girl. We both had executive jobs – he was at KPMG, I was at the BBC – and between us, we pulled in a juicy six-figure salary that paid for five holidays a year and an enviable lifestyle. Life was good. Tony was a kind, gentle man, and in our short time together he showed me what it was to be loved completely. He stood by as I chased my dreams, understanding that I was ambitious and that I measured happiness by success and needed to fill every moment with doing. I was a superwoman with a tick list as long as my arm: Run the London Marathon – tick (I crawled round in 2007); have a baby – tick (our beautiful son, Fionn, was born on 7th August 2008); get a degree – tick (I got my Masters in Business Administration in 2009 while also working full-time at the BBC). Life was good.

Tony used to bring our son to business school in between lectures so that I could breastfeed – I was unstoppable. And when I completed everything, he asked, "What next, Dee? Isn't it time to just live?" I don't know, perhaps he could see what was coming. We finished renovations on our dream house on 25th June 2010; it was the final tick. The next day he was dead. In the blink of an eye, our life together was over before we had even really got started. I had achieved so much, but what for? My beautiful husband was gone and I was left to pick up the pieces.

I put on the veil, shut myself down and went back to work after two short months. I was determined that grief wouldn't define me. You see, I had been there the year before. Martyn, my daughter's father, had killed himself on 21st March 2009. I had dealt with the loss then; I could deal with this now. But losing Martyn was Millie's pain, not mine. Martyn and I may have had a daughter together but we had separated long ago, he didn't live in my heart as Tony did. Losing Tony was like losing myself, and my whole existence became blurred. I felt like this terrible dark cloud had penetrated every cell of my body, and with it came a wave of anger that was raw and unforgiving. How could God do this to me? Tony was meant to be my happy ever after; this hadn't been part of the fucking plan! I was resentful of other people's happiness, and I had a desperate need to numb the pain, running from it through an increasing reliance on alcohol and a string of bad relationships that left me questioning my judgement and added more suffering to my life. And yet there was another cruel twist to come. In 2011, our little baby boy Fionn was diagnosed with cerebral palsy, just a year after Tony's death. I blamed myself entirely for his condition, because I had ruptured my placenta while gardening when I was 29 weeks pregnant, and my son's brain had been starved of oxygen. My anger now had a fresh target, and I had an almighty fight on my hands to accept my little boy's condition and to forgive myself for his health problems.

My soul was bleeding. My everyday life had become such a burden that it was difficult to see out of the fog and find the light, but somehow, through it all, I was determined to shine. And so, I started to put my life back together one tiny step at a time, and I did this by practising yoga on a daily basis and reading every spiritual book I could get my hands on. I became a yoga teacher, gave up the BBC job in 2011 and taught yoga for three years, but something was missing. I was still trying to control life, and I felt stuck and exhausted. And there was yet still more to come. A third partner Paul, who I had dated briefly for 2 years died unexpectedly in 2014. He was a secret alcoholic, and I walked out of that relationship 3 months pregnant knowing that I could not keep the baby. I made the agonising decision to return my unborn child to Spirit and buried all the shame and guilt deep into the recesses of my womb. But when Paul died the embers of suffering started to feed my soul. His death was yet another nail in the coffin, if you pardon the pun, that sent me on a downward spiral of questioning and self-loathing. Suddenly, I was faced with the shocking reality that I had 2 children, and a child in spirit by 3 fathers and they were all dead. All young men in their 40s, they had all died suddenly and unexpectedly in what should have been the prime of their lives. And they were all connected to me. How could this be? It seemed that death had a way of finding me and was clearly trying to teach me something about life but at the time I just didn't understand what it could be. My soul was utterly wounded by my story, by the trinity of death that crossed my path, and I felt ashamed, damaged and somehow cursed as a new level of darkness entered my world and consumed my very being.

Then, on 21st March 2015, I stopped. I'd had enough. I was on my knees and broken as I looked to the heavens and cried, "I can't do this anymore, what am I supposed to do?" It was at this moment that I got out my pen and notebook and started to write. I had this feeling that I can only describe as an inner knowing; a voice that has always been there to guide me, but one I had ignored through my own pain and suffering. And now she was calling out to be heard. She is the wisdom within who never gives up on us. As she whispered, "Write, Dee, you must write every day," I gave my trust to her and followed her guidance. In the beginning, it was agonisingly hard to sit at my desk staring into the abyss of my soul's story, the sadness in my heart penetrated every word on the page. Despite how difficult it was, I kept the faith and carried on writing. In the moments of sadness, I felt the divine wisdom hold my heart as she whispered, "It's OK, Dee, it's going to be OK."

This beautiful voice of the Divine that started to flow through my words had a plan for me. She was calling me to write my story for a higher purpose that was beyond my understanding at the time. She was calling me to be healed, and as I cried a thousand tears onto the pages, I opened my heart and finally let go of all the pain and suffering I had carried for years. I could feel the healing light of love in my heart and, as I awakened to its presence, it became increasingly clear that I had been guided by a divine truth all my life; a truth that showed itself the night before Tony died and was there to protect and prepare me for the road ahead. This truth is connected to the inner light inside us all, if only we had eyes that could see and ears that could hear it. There is only one truth, but there are many paths to it, and here in my story, I share with you mine.

Chapter 2

Growing Up

———————————— ❖ ————————————

"It takes courage to grow up and become who you really are."

I was born into a world of love and confusion. It was a world of conformity, Catholicism and pleasing others, where being seen to do the right thing was everything. My father was lost to drink and my mother raised four children without complaining, doing her best out of duty and necessity, as she buried her dreams and made the most of her lot. My birth name was Dolores Ann Fallon. It was a name that made me cringe, and a name that I always denied. I never really understood why, until years later, when I realised how disconnected I was from this world that I had chosen to enter. "Your father should never have married," was Mum's opening line whenever we discussed the past and his downfalls. She was just 17 when she fell pregnant with my twin brothers, Adrian and Patrick, and both she and my dad were sent to England to get married, as having children out of wedlock in 1960s Ireland was not the done thing. A year later, my sister Susan was born and I arrived a year after that - on 30th May 1969. This all happened before Mum hit 20 and she raised the four of us pretty much singlehandedly. My dad, Patsy Fallon, was, by his own admission, a lovable rogue. He was happiest when he was propping up a bar telling his famous stories to any passing waif or stray. Charismatic, intelligent and generous, everybody loved Patsy. In the 70s and 80s, he ran his own successful building company and employed lots of local men. He was a central figure in the Irish community in our hometown of Watford in the UK and was heavily involved in Gaelic hurling and football. I was raised with strong, working-class Irish values, to work hard, show good manners and obey our mother. We were punished if we failed to do as we were told. This didn't involve anything too brutal, there was the odd slap or strike with the back of a slipper, but it definitely reminded me of my place in life. As the youngest in the family, I also knew I was last in the pecking order.

Life in our household was very routine. During the week, Mum would cook the exact same food. Monday was stew, Tuesday was bacon and cabbage, Wednesday was chicken, Thursday was a fry up and Friday was fish and chips. Saturday was, as she put it, her 'day off' so she didn't cook a hot meal. Instead, she would bake the most delicious cakes, scones and 'mammie's soda bread' and we would have filled rolls from the bakery. Sunday was a big roast dinner. Week in, week out, it was always the same. Meals were served at 6 pm, except on Sunday when the roast was dished up at 3 pm. You could set your watch by it. And boy did I love my mum's dinners. She was a fantastic cook and we always ate every morsel on our plates. There was no other food or snacks in the house so we either ate what was given to us or went hungry. Dad worked six days a week and went to the pub every day without fail. Mum would leave his dinner sitting on the side and he'd eat it when he came home, by which time we'd all be in bed. On Saturday night we all went to the Irish club. Dad would prop up the bar and Mum would dance the night away with her friends. I cherished those Saturday evenings. I loved to spin around the dance floor doing the waltz or twist and turn like a lightning bolt while taking part in a jive. On Sundays, we slightly begrudgingly went to mass. We were not a particularly religious family and I was never encouraged to pray at bedtime or read the Bible, but we had to be 'seen' at church.

"Make sure the priest sees you," Mum would say.

Attending mass was her way of showing the world she was doing a good job and raising her children in the Catholic faith, which was important to her. Dad was less bothered. He'd go if he felt like it, or if Mum made him, but he didn't care so much about being seen to be doing the right thing. Sunday afternoon was the highlight of my week as we visited our extended family for tea and cake in Luton, the town next to ours. It was a rare moment of family unity and was a chance for me to be a child again as I played with my cousins and watched my mum looking happy for a few short hours as she caught up with her four sisters. This was also a way of getting Dad away from the pub and being a real father. He had to take us to Luton in his green work van - which we aptly named 'The Green Goddess' - because mum couldn't drive and catching the bus with four children was not her idea of a fun afternoon out. However, she had to beg him every week to take us. His reluctance wasn't because he didn't enjoy spending time with his family, but because he didn't like being too far away from the pub. We would arrive around 4 pm and an hour and a half later he would be getting restless and trying to gather us all up to leave. Then he would drive at lightning speed down the motorway in time for opening hours. On Monday, Dad would head to work at 6 am and then go straight to the pub until closing time, losing himself in drink once again. And that was our family life. My dad wasn't unkind, aggressive or difficult, he was simply lost to his love of booze. I felt that loss deeply in my heart and wanted him to be different. I wanted my dad to be 'normal' and, as I grew older and compared my life to the lives of my friends, I developed a very clear sense of what I thought 'normal' should be. I wanted a dad who came home from work early, gave me cuddles without the accompanying smell of stale beer, read me a story at bedtime, tucked me up, told me he loved me, took an interest in my education and wanted to teach me to ride a bike. This person didn't have to be extraordinary in any way. He just had to want to do 'dad' things.

> "A mother is truly Divine. It is from her womb that we have emerged... this means treating her with respect, with love, with patience."[2]

Mum rarely showed how desperately sad she was, despite spending many a night crying herself to sleep and looking out of the window wondering where her husband was. She was a silent martyr and cared for and loved us with everything she had. We were her world and her pride and joy, and somehow, I turned into a silent martyr just like her. I could see she was struggling so I wanted to ease her burden. I became the good girl who helped in the house and cleaned up after everyone when she was too exhausted to do it. I also dragged the weekly shopping home from town because Dad was never around to help her. I stepped in where he should have been. And I did the same for him. I helped him with his business accounts and paperwork when it got out of control, which it often did. It was as if I'd been propelled into the family to be of service. I never complained, but I watched on in silent judgement, as my inner voice questioned everything around me. I hid my true feelings behind an innocent smile that just accepted that this was how life was. I was never encouraged to speak my mind or be ambitious. Life was about getting through the drudgery of day-to-day existence. Money – namely the lack of it – was always an issue. Once we were at school, Mum took a job as a dinner lady so she'd have a bit of pocket money – Dad was never that reliable with the finances. I attended a good Roman Catholic school run by nuns. They were heavy-handed on the discipline front and would punish us if our skirts weren't below the knee or if our hair wasn't neatly kept. I was terrified of the church and the Catholic doctrine that had been fed to me since birth. I always winced when I looked up at Jesus on the cross and questioned the loving nature of God, especially when one of the nuns pulled my hair to silence me if she felt I was being too proud or loud. How could they be considered honourable when they behaved in such a way? There was so much judgement and double standards in the church, but I dutifully attended mass and swallowed the words of the Bible without ever fully believing in them.

Despite taking on a part-time job, Mum never had any spare cash to buy us little extras. We were not poor by any standard, but when I went to school and saw where all the other kids lived and how they had bikes and music lessons and nice holidays and went to restaurants with their parents, I started to see a life that I wanted. I wanted a middle-class life like all my friends, not the working-class one I had. I felt embarrassed by our little two-up two-down terrace, which was tiny compared with my contemporaries' beautiful suburban semis. And I judged myself as not being worthy of their friendship. I kept to myself and was never invited over for sleepovers; I began to isolate myself and nurture my growing lack of self-worth. This sense of not feeling good enough shaped my whole teenage years and had a huge impact on my relationships with others, particularly men. I remember once pleading with my mum to pay for ballet lessons, but she couldn't afford them. She could see how upset I was as I watched my friends skip off in their beautiful pink tutus and I know this weighed heavily on her – no parent wants to see their child miss out. She wanted to give us the best, but what could she do? She grew up at a time when women lacked financial freedom. They married young, often out of necessity, and were expected to stay at home with the children while the 'man of the house' basically went about his business as he pleased. Mum's own mother lived that way, as did her grandmother and no doubt countless other women down her family line. This was just how it was. But the path Mum was on wasn't the one she wanted for her daughters.

"You must always have your own money," she'd remind us whenever she could. "Don't ever rely on a man."

It was too late for her to live by that mantra, but her advice certainly helped to shape me into the woman I am today. I have a generation of Jackson women to thank for my fierce independence and my desire to be self-sufficient come what may. And so, the struggles in my teenage years planted the seed for the life I wanted: the middle-class life that my school friends had, with the nice house, the 2.4 kids and the professional husband. I was determined to be the one to break the mould and close the door on the emotional turmoil of the life I'd been born into.

Meanwhile, Mum didn't feel she had the strength to make a change and remained in her marriage for 20 years. Throughout this whole period, she was nursing a broken heart. When we kids were little, she had met a man at the Irish club and had fallen desperately in love. This man was also married with a young family, and although they pined to be together, neither could face the prospect of breaking up their respective lives. So, they agreed to 'do the right thing' by sacrificing their own happiness and staying away from each other. Their paths crossed frequently – the Irish community in Watford was a tight circle of people – and it must have been so difficult for them to resign themselves to separate married lives while being so desperately in love. But they couldn't live out the pretence forever – love always finds a way to surface – and by the time I was 18, Mum's marriage to Dad had started to implode. She'd had enough. Dad's drinking had become increasingly out of control, and in the last few years of their time together he just seemed to give up. Bills remained unpaid, the house was close to being repossessed and his building business went bankrupt. Mum didn't want to know. She'd pretty much given up too. She made her mind up that she'd paid her dues and now it was time for her to find some happiness.

She saw my coming of age, her youngest child, as her gateway to freedom. Throughout the darkest days of her marriage, she had promised herself she would stick with my dad through it all, but only until her children were all old enough to stand on their own two feet. For her, that time came when I reached adulthood. And, although I was still at college and needed my mum, the inner strength she saw in me gave her the confidence to start a new life.

While my brothers and sister were working and had lives outside of the house and long-term partners to turn to, I was on my own. Mum had threatened to go many times, and even packed her bags and left, only to return 30 minutes later after missing her bus. This time, though, there was no turning back. She was terrified of what her family and the church would say and didn't know how she would cope being on her own. She used to come up to my bed late at night, cry on my shoulder and seek my advice. I never once thought about the impact this was having on me, I simply sat, listened and provided comfort. Mum was like a little child. I could see that her fear ran deep, but I also empathised with her need to find happiness. She used to say I was more like a mother to her than she was to me. With just the clothes on her back, she was scared and lonely, but she finally had her freedom. This came at a price, though, and in those early days, after she left, Mum had many dark moments as she battled with guilt, carrying the shame of a generation of women who did the unthinkable and left their husbands and families. Inevitably, the struggle took its toll on her health, but she eventually grew stronger and never gave up on romance. She was finally free to be with the man she had fallen in love with all those years earlier. They settled together in Ireland and lived in a house two doors down from where Mum grew up and spent over 30 years together until he died peacefully in his sleep at the age of 80. My lovely mum felt the pains of grief that I could see etched on her face because she had learnt to love so deeply. And whilst I wish she didn't feel the longing that I knew only too well, I know it's because she was able to love this man with all her heart, and this is a price worth paying.

Dad was furious when Mum left. He never actually believed she would do it, despite her years spent threatening to, and he just wasn't ready to accept responsibility for himself, so he directed his anger at me. He blamed me for helping her leave and in a fit of rage kicked me out of the house, telling me he never wanted to see me again. He seemed to have forgotten the nights I'd held him as he cried on my shoulder in drunken despair, knowing the marriage was over. Instead of gratitude for my help, there I was at 19, in the middle of my college exams, with an absent mum and a dad who had made me homeless. I was on my own and had been abandoned by the two people in the world on who I should have been able to rely. It felt as if everything was falling apart around me. My siblings, who had never known about Mum's intention to leave, were deeply shocked, and they dealt with their pain in their own separate ways. Adrian and Susan had moved out to live with their partners and get on with their lives while Patrick stayed with Dad and tried to steady the ship before the inevitable happened and the house was repossessed. Without Mum to pull us all together, our family just sort of disintegrated. I saw very little of my brothers and sister in those early days after she left. Dad hit the bottle hard and refused to speak to me, despite my efforts to hold out an olive branch and make some peace. Mum also went off the radar for a while. She needed time alone to grieve for her marriage and family, and to pick over the pieces of her life as she tried to make sense of what had gone wrong. And so, for the first time in my life, I was on my own.

With very little money, I moved to London to start a new life. For a while, I moved about a lot. The worst place I stayed was a squat in Brixton, south London. It was freezing cold, had no running water and the boys I shared with organised impromptu raves and trashed the place – not that there was much to trash. It was a pretty grim time. I eventually moved to a comfortable flat in Islington, got a job at an advertising agency and worked hard to provide for myself. But as someone who learnt how to love through helping others, I became desperate to please and struggled with setting boundaries I found it hard to stand my ground at work and say no, so I ended up doing more than my fair share of long hours and early mornings, which eventually took a physical toll on me. I became resentful of work and hated living in London. I had never felt so lonely or lost in my entire life. When my work colleagues left in the evening to be with their families, it only reminded me how I didn't have anywhere to call home. At the time, I didn't know how to express my feelings or talk about my past. I kept my parents' ugly separation a secret and covered up just how much I was hurting inside. Without that strong foundation of family love and support, I struggled to know how to say enough was enough. Instead, I lived behind the façade of my carefully constructed persona – and she needed to be perfect. During a two-year stint of excessive exercise and bulimic purging, I forced my body into being a perfect size 8. I was in a constant state of anger, sadness and frustration, and I turned these emotions on myself as I abused my body. It was a horrendous time. I felt I was going insane and was ashamed about what I was doing to myself, which only fed into my cycle of self-loathing. There was no space to breathe. I strictly controlled calorie intake before trying to burn them off with three hours of running, swimming and cycling followed by another purge to make sure nothing stayed in my system. Being bulimic is a truly horrifying way to live and by the time I was 21, the tortuous hours of exercise and constant control of my diet had taken their toll and I was almost at breaking point. I gave up my job at the ad agency and went to stay with Mum, who at this time was living close to her sisters in Luton. I trained to become a croupier at the local casino and saved every penny to go travelling, which I saw as my big 'way out'.

Meanwhile, I continued to be consumed with hatred. I hated living in Luton and was desperately unhappy. I carried on with my gruelling training sessions for another six months before coming home one day and breaking down.

"I can't do this anymore," I screamed at mum.

She couldn't hide her shock. She had never seen me vulnerable, and suddenly here I was broken for the first time. I'd given up the façade and self-control and for the first time in years, I let the anger surface and asked for help. In the summer of 1990, I went to see a therapist. As I opened up, her response spoke directly to my soul.

"Dee you're an adult now and you make mistakes and that's OK," she said. *"Your parents are also adults and they make mistakes too."*

Her words really resonated with me. I knew I was being called to show compassion and forgiveness to my parents for my childhood experiences. And to some extent I did. But I failed to see this message was actually a call for me to make peace with myself. It was an opportunity for me to grow up, release my resentment and anger and move on. Unfortunately, I was still stuck in a pattern of looking outwards. I lived behind the veil of the good girl and fixated on helping others, dishing out advice and judging people. It was only when I had therapy again years later that I learnt how my behaviour was a coping mechanism to try and control life, and I'd actually been in deep denial about my childhood and still held onto many painful feelings that needed to be released.

After seeing the therapist, I decided I wanted to try to make amends with my dad. I was about to go travelling and decided to see him before I left. We met in a local pub and he looked a bit sheepish. I think he was probably hungover from the night before. Rather naively, the first thing he said to me was, "You've put on a bit of weight, Dolores."

OMG! The man hadn't seen me for two years and the first thing he did was call me fat. I was utterly floored. I mean, really, surely all men know they're walking into dangerous territory if they comment on a woman's weight, let alone a woman who is recovering from bulimia? But Dad wasn't aware of the pain that sat behind my excess pounds – he didn't know about my bulimia and my struggles. He hadn't been around to help me through that tough time in my life and his words lit the fuse that triggered the bomb inside me that had been waiting to explode. Boy did I let him have it. In an explosive rage of pure hatred and judgement, I spewed out a list of crimes as I told him what a useless father he was, and how he had constantly let me down, disappointed me, embarrassed me, and so on. He listened gobsmacked as I hurled abuse after abuse until the fire inside me had burnt out.

As a finishing remark, I looked him in the eye and said, "You haven't been the best of dads, but despite it all I love you and I forgive you."

How very big of me after I had pulled the man to pieces. That was my idea of empathy at the time. Castrate the man then say, "It's OK, I forgive you."

To his credit, Dad didn't walk away and when I had finished talking, he looked at me rather solemnly and replied, "You always were the strong one. I wish your mother had stood up to me as you did."

But I was hiding behind my strength. Being strong was my coping mechanism. I put all the hurt and sadness from my childhood into a box, locked it away and got on with life. In many ways, I was no different from Dad. He hid behind alcohol to ease the pain, while I hid behind strength. But, as I was to discover 25 years later when I had therapy again, whatever we lock away has to eventually find its way out.

So, at the age of 21, I closed the door on my past and backpacked around India, South East Asia and Australia to escape my misery, essentially staying on the road until I was 25. It was then that my love affair with India began. I only came back to the UK once during that period because I'd run out of money. Once home, I took on three jobs and worked every hour God sent, putting my life on hold till I'd saved up enough to be able to return to India six months later. It was where I needed to be.

Chapter 3

Moving On

❖

"Our bodies and our brains may be in the West, but our spirit must stay with our motherland, in India."[3]

I first stepped on Indian soil after arriving in New Delhi at 4 am on a British Airways flight. I was with my friend Donna and we were absolutely bloody terrified. Landing anywhere new at 4 am is never a smart move, especially when you are two young British girls and look squeaky clean and very green. We were both 21 and had never been outside Europe before. It didn't help that back in the 1990s, everyone in India seemed to be out to scam you. Whenever you arrived somewhere new, you'd hear news of a curfew or, "No, Madame, there is no electricity," or, "No, Madame, there is holiday, nothing is open," or, "No, Madame, there is fighting between Hindus and Muslims, it's not safe. You have to come with me and I take you to the best hotel!"

Each city had its own unique way of trying to fleece the unsuspecting tourist. Over time we became savvier to these tricks. We grew in confidence and looked noticeably dirtier – as you do when you backpack around India. On the plus side, the dirtier we got the more the scammers left us alone.

When we arrived in Delhi on that first morning, we were told there was a curfew and the city was on lockdown, which meant we couldn't go to our youth hostel. The taxi drivers wanted to take us to a fancy hotel that would have blown our monthly budget in one fell swoop and left them rich in the pocket after receiving a backhander from the hotel owner. All they could see were two rich, Western tourists, who between them had more money than they could possibly earn in a lifetime – and they wanted a piece of it.

I gathered some inner strength, took Donna's hand and hustled our way through the crowds and onto a local bus, which took us to the area where the youth hostel was. Needless to say, it was in the middle of nowhere. The bus driver dropped us off in the darkness of the night and said something in Hindi, which I can only assume was along the lines of, "Do you really want to stay here in the arse end of nowhere?"

I'm sure Donna was thinking the same thing, but in my mind, we were intrepid explorers and I was damned if a little hiccup like a curfew was going to scupper my plans for adventure. And that's how we made our way around magical India – with a large dose of faith that all would be well and a carefree attitude that brought us the most vivid, amazing and spellbinding experiences I can still practically touch today. I fell in love – India was my country. I belonged to her and she belonged to me. I knew deeply that part of me had walked with her in a previous life and I felt guided by an Indian spirit. I had this longing for a woman who lived in colonial India, at the time of British rule. I felt her energy with me as if she was me in another life.

I was 22 when I went back to India for the second time. This time I was on my own, just me and my backpack, and I loved the freedom of it all. Suddenly I had nobody else to please but myself. But of course, I was never really on my own for long. Backpackers follow a well-trodden route around India, searching out the hashish and party scene, as well as the temples and culture. And so, I ended up travelling in a convoy of 20 people, all from different nationalities. We were all doing our own thing but ended up following each other along the path. We spent most of our time in the temples and on the beaches of Southern India, and for the first time in my life, I felt truly happy. I was comfortable in my skin, had locked away the pain of my childhood and was finally enjoying living my freedom and caring only for myself. And, of course, I was stoned most of the time! I used to wake up to a chillum and smoke my way through the day as I glided around India on a haze of hashish, experiencing life in technicolour, and doing some crazy ass shit. I gave away all my possessions in Madura as an act of blissful detachment from materialism. I still vividly remember standing at the temple complex giving my precious Sony Walkman to the street kids and declaring I no longer needed it because I was free – I must have been really stoned that day! I camped out under the stars on Om beach in Gokarna and lived for three weeks in a hut that I'd constructed out of bamboo. I drank chai, smoked hash and swam with the dolphins at sunset. Back then, the beaches in the south were little bits of uncommercialised paradises and it was just me and my group of friends and the chai man. We travelled with our own stove and chapatti pan and would pitch up on a beach, make a fire, cook food, watch the sunset and laze around for days. I hung out at the legendary Shore Bar in Anjuna, North Goa, for months and haggled with the Rajasthani women at the Wednesday flea market, becoming part of the hippie scene and buying my drugs from a guy called Neptune who looked like he was still on a trip from the 60s. I was always level-headed enough to dip in, experiment and have my fun while knowing when it was time to take myself away. I saw too many casualties of that scene to want to do that to myself. I witnessed many Israelis party hard just to anesthetise the memory of military service only to lose themselves to heroin and acid and add more suffering.

In the village of Mahabalipurumm in Tamil Nadu, I lived in a hut made out of cow dung and had to take a stick with me to keep the pigs at bay when I went to the toilet in the field outside. I also climbed the giant boulders and explored the forlorn ruins of Hampi, which I can only describe as out of this world – to the point where I believe the gods must have had some involvement in its creation. I watched phosphorus dance in the moonlight whilst gliding down the Keralan backwaters on a houseboat, and I walked through the monsoon-soaked streets of Calcutta with water up to my knees, trying not to think of what was lurking in the soup around my ankles. India left its imprint on my heart and when it was time to leave, I cried like a baby. I remember sitting on the airport floor in Calcutta and sobbing as I waited for a flight to Hong Kong, wondering when I'd be back. Little did I know it would take 25 years for me to step on Indian soil again, but when I did the country held out her arms and embraced my heart once again. It was worth the wait.

"In the sweetness of friendship let there be laughter, and sharing of pleasures. For in the dew of little things the heart finds its morning and is refreshed."

– Khalil Gibran

Between the ages of 23 and 25, I lived in Hong Kong and Australia and worked as a waitress in various bars and restaurants to feed my travelling lifestyle. While in Hong Kong, I met my lifelong best friend, Debbie. She was the first woman I had ever grown close to and loved. Her energy, zest for life and passion to party is the stuff of legend. She's been with me every step of the way since we met, guiding me through the rough and the smooth. She was a bridesmaid at my wedding, was the first to visit me when the kids were born and held my hand when Tony died, wiping away my tears and looking after me through the dark times. She never questioned or judged when my behaviour spiralled out of control but was always there in the background to pick me up when I was ready to fall. She was the best friend I'd always wanted when I was a little girl. Back then I was the child on the outside looking in. I had never really connected with anyone on a deep level, had a best friend to do girly things with or go for sleepovers. But when I met Debbie all that changed and I couldn't have asked for a better friend. I truly believe the universe gives you everything you need in its own divine time. We've celebrated three milestone birthdays (our 30th, 40th and 50th) together, and I know we'll be doing the same for the rest of our days. I'm truly grateful for the gift of her friendship. There are very few people in life that are with you every step of the way, and when we find them it's a real blessing. People come in and out of our lives for all sorts of reasons, but there is something special about a male or female friendship that endures over time. There is safety in it. For me, there is space to be me. It's a chance to come off the stage, let go of the jazz hands and be authentic.

I will also always be truly grateful for having the means and the desire to want to travel, especially when half the world lives hand to mouth and will never enjoy the same opportunities. I am reminded of that every time I am in Asia, where most people live day to day, and some never get to leave their local area, let alone step outside their country to experience life elsewhere. So, I count my blessings every time I go off on an adventure. Travel feeds my soul. I always come back from a trip a better, more conscious and a humbler human being.

Chapter 4

Then There Were Three

"Only I can change my life. No one can do it for me."
- Carol Burnett

My first child Millie was born on 5th March 1998, and it was love at first sight. She was the child I had wanted and longed for since I was little when all I had ever dreamt about was getting married and having children. I used to dream about her as a way of escaping the turmoil that was going on inside me as I grew up. In my dreams, I was 25 and living in middle-class suburbia in a beautiful house with a dutiful husband who provided for my two children and me. It was the antithesis of the life I had growing up. I craved a stable home environment and all I ever wanted in life was to get married and start a family. When I hit 25, I came back from my travels and set about fulfilling my dream. I wanted to find a husband to settle down with and get married to. Well of sorts. That was the master plan, the place I was always heading towards, but I wasn't yet done with the party scene and having fun. I worked hard in the ad agency by day and sipped vast quantities of Chardonnay by night with my work friends - it was the 1990s after all. At the weekend I would hit it hard with the friends I'd met travelling. We were all back in London, living in denial and still not quite ready to leave the party. We used to head out to the Chunnel Club on Saturday nights, high on life and ecstasy, and see it through to Sunday, welcoming in the dawn of a new day by dancing away to hardcore trance music at Strawberry Sundays with a legion of other like-minded travellers. We were reminiscing about the full moon parties of Koh Phangan and trying to recreate the magic in a sweaty club under the arches of Vauxhall Bridge in South London. This was how my life rolled. I had a foot in two camps and felt equally comfortable in both. Part of me was drawn to the bright lights of London and the heady experience of metropolitan living, which included a big job, money, a beautiful house, a fancy car, beautiful clothes and the *Sex in the City* lifestyle that saw me as a girl about town in the best bars and restaurants. But another part of me wanted to be barefoot and dirty in the sand with all the travellers and alternative people who lived at the other extreme. They were the people who lived outside the system – a creative, artsy alternative crew who wouldn't be seen dead inside an office pen-pushing to feed the corporate machine. They lived for the festival scene, worked for charities or made their money through their art, or by doing a meaningful job that balanced their karma and contributed to making the world a better place to be. Martyn, Millie's dad, was one of those people. I met him at a house party in Maida Vale that had been thrown by some friends from Hong Kong, and the attraction was instant. We got together in a haze of drink and drugs in the summer of 1996, partied the weekends away until the twilight hours and limped through the working week in eager anticipation to repeat it all again the following Friday and Saturday. That was our life together until I got pregnant and had to grow up. Martyn, on the other hand, was the boy who never grew up. He bounced around with an exuberant laugh and a zest for life that was extreme. He did everything to the max. He ate too much, drank too much and smoked too much, but he also laughed for England and was as playful as a puppy and great fun to be around. Well, he was when he was on a high. He also tended to swing the other way and his life was plagued by bouts of deep depression that kept him trapped in a dark place. He worked for a charity to help rehouse homeless people and was very passionate about fixing the social injustice in the UK. He saw how the rich were getting richer while the less fortunate in society were downtrodden. He was a complete socialist lefty who believed in taxing the rich to feed the poor, and he hated the inequality of the world, which favoured white, middle-class men. He was a freedom fighter for the rights of the underprivileged. He stood up for women's rights, gay rights and the rights of the homeless. His heart was in the right place but his mind was very complex. He struggled with his demons. His friends were all similar. They were struggling artists and musicians, or they were unemployed, but they were all cut from the same cloth and wanted to live outside the system. And in some ways that was the appeal of our union. Martyn was a great antidote to the corporate life that was filling my pockets and broadening my waistband but failing to feed my soul. It was a whirlwind romance: we met, fell in love and moved in with each other within three months. I think this was more out of necessity than anything else, he had nowhere to live and was sofa surfing. But I knew, from the moment I found out I was pregnant that my relationship wasn't going to last because it was held together by a haze of drink and drugs. The highs were very high but the lows were very low, and in the cold light of day, when I stepped out of that lifestyle due to my condition, I saw clearly that we weren't well matched. Five months into my pregnancy, I remember sobbing into Debbie's arm, as I knew I would be bringing up my daughter on my own. This was not part of the dream, the little girl's vision of happiness. I was unmarried, 20 weeks pregnant and living in a small, rented shared flat in North West London with a man I didn't love. This was actually my worst nightmare, and it was also Martyn's. I think we both knew that the relationship was never going to work, but we held on until Millie was born and stayed together for nine months afterwards as we battled with ourselves and the reality of our situation. And that reality was not pretty. Martyn was unemployed and looked after Millie full-time while I went back to work at the ad agency to provide for us. This was not how it was supposed to be. I was meant to be married and living in a nice house with my husband supporting me. Ours was not a balanced relationship, and our union was all over and done with by January 1999. Martyn went back to his hometown of Norwich, and I went to live in Luton to be close to my family. After the initial unpleasantness that comes with a separation and two years of fighting in court, which bled us dry both financially and emotionally, we eventually found our peace and became friends.

Millie is very much her father's daughter. She absolutely adored her larger-than-life dad. Her stays with him at weekends and for extended periods in the holidays were always filled with tales of great mischief. He made a big impression on her life, and although his mental health was not always stable, he firmly believed that he was put on this earth to help others. He was passionate about helping the homeless and ironically his motto was, "All you need is love." Unfortunately, he never quite lived that truth for himself.

"It is not death that man should fear, he should fear never beginning to live."

– Marcus Aurelius

Martyn's life came to a tragic end on 21st March 2009. He suffered from bipolar disorder and ended his life by taking a massive overdose of his prescribed medication, enough to knock out a horse three times over. He looked like he meant it. The police called me late Saturday evening on 22nd March to confirm his death, and although they had to wait for the coroner's report, they alluded to the fact that he had taken his own life. My beautiful little Millie was upstairs happily asleep in bed, and the next morning I knew I'd have to break the devastating news to a sweet, gentle 11-year-old girl that her beloved daddy had died. How does a person do that? I remember spending the night shaking with fear. I was so scared of the hurt and pain I was about to bring to her and fearful of what words to choose. I didn't know how to say it was suicide. How would I explain to a little child that an adult could be so desperate and so unhappy that they might want to take their own life? How could I bring reason, logic and compassion to something that I could barely comprehend myself? And worse of all, I knew what I had to do would break her spirit.

The next day was Mothering Sunday and, bless her, Millie hopped into my bedroom all excited to give me my present and make me breakfast in bed. Instead, I had to sit her down and tell her the worst news imaginable. I will never ever forget that moment. The shock on her face, the moment of denial, the moment of questioning – "No, it can't be true, Mummy, it can't be possible" – and then the soul-shattering moment of reality when she realised it was true and let out a heart-bursting, guttural scream that pierced my very being. I've only ever heard that scream one other time before, and it came from my soul the day my Tony died.

"Be Western (if you live in the West) when it comes to professional excellence but be Indian in your domestic life and in your heart."[4]

I joined the BBC at the same time as my relationship with Martyn ended, remaining there for 14 years. I had to find a way of juggling work, commuting and being a single mum. Before joining the BBC, I was working round the clock in advertising agencies but there was no way I could sustain a media lifestyle with a new-born child. I couldn't just get up and leave the office every day at 5 pm while my team worked late into the night (which was common practice at ad agencies back in the 90s). And I wasn't prepared to compromise spending time at home with my daughter in the evenings. She was just too precious for that. Advertising wasn't your average nine to five kind of job and I was the first working mum at the agency and at the time I had to break down barriers to get a four-day week contract. Everyone said the agency would never give the contract to me, but they did. I'm proud to have played a part in setting the way for other working mums at the agency, but I hated walking out of the door at 5 pm, and I hated missing out on all the social events that went hand-in-hand with my job, such as popping over the road to the local pub for a post-work drink and a chinwag or going out on numerous corporate events, or jollies as we used to call them. This was very much part of the ad scene back in the 1990s. So, when I stumbled across the ad for the job at the BBC in the *Media Guardian*, I put an application in at the last minute and thought nothing of it. And much to my surprise, I got the job. I was the perfect candidate for the role, but dare I say, I think I might have been the only candidate who applied! But I came at a price. I wasn't prepared to move without getting what I wanted. So, I asked for a 25% pay increase, a four-day working week, and an understanding that I would leave work at 5 pm every day. I insisted they gave me access to the network so I could work from home one day a week, and I basically wanted to keep my own schedule. It was a pretty ballsy move because in truth I wasn't attached to the outcome, I had a perfectly good job, so I had nothing to lose. I figured I could stand my ground and ask for what I wanted. And they acquiesced to all my demands. Working at the BBC was a huge blessing when it came to the minefield that was being a working mum in the 1990s. I'm sure a lot of women will understand when I say I constantly felt compromised for wanting to have a meaningful career whilst wishing to spend quality time at home raising my daughter. I grew up with feminism as my standard and a culture that was almost insistent that women should go out to work and prove themselves. My peers and I couldn't be content with staying at home, having babies and being supported by our husbands. That would have been a real crime back in my day. We had to pave the way for a generation of women and show the world we could have it all. It was a badge of honour to the sisterhood to be absolutely on your knees and ravaged with exhaustion as you held down a full-time power job, raised 2.4 perfect kids, cooked a Michelin-starred meal for the hubby, arranged a full social life for the kids after school, with activities such as Mandarin and violin lessons, and planned culturally enriching weekends for the grownups, including trips to the theatre and wine tasting. I'm bloody exhausted just thinking about it. But this is how I lived my life back then. I was on the conveyer belt of doing and achieving so much on the outside, but I had little conscious awareness of what was happening on the inside. I was driven by ambition, and if I'm honest I measured my happiness in money, achievement and fitting in with the social norm. And anyway, I had very little choice in the early days. I was a single mum with a child to raise and a mortgage to pay.

Although I loved my work, those early years of Millie's life were very difficult. I hated living in Luton and I hated being on my own. It was a very dark time. I never wanted to be a single mum, and here I was at 30 living in a town I had fled nearly a decade earlier. I felt like I was back at the beginning, and I was deeply wounded. How could this be? This wasn't part of the plan. My Catholic upbringing had left me feeling very ashamed of my single-mum status, and my lack of self-worth and the issues from my childhood still lurked deep inside my soul and were calling to be healed. I wanted nothing more than to meet a nice man to take me away from it all and support my daughter and me. But we don't attract nice men when we are in the depths of darkness – we attract the not-so-nice men, and believe it or not it was my father who introduced me to the next one, and that relationship turned out to be an absolute disaster. I should have known really. He was a secret alcoholic just like my dad. Another wounded soul I tried to fix. Everyone around me at the time knew the relationship was all wrong, as did I, but somehow being with him seemed better than being on my own. It wasn't. He hid behind his alcohol addiction, which he managed to keep a secret for 18 months, or maybe I just didn't want to see it. Then, one day, I got into the car with him, his two daughters and Millie, and he was so drunk that he could barely keep the car on the road. I managed to pull the steering wheel out of his hands and swerve the car onto a grass verge, as we were about to approach a busy motorway. It was a very dark time for me and I was also 3 months pregnant with his child, but the near-accident gave me the strength to leave and we parted company that day and I never saw him again. Paul never recovered from his addictions and he died in 2014 from an alcohol-related illness. He was in his mid-40s.

I decided not to keep the baby, and I locked away the shame and guilt of that time in the deepest, darkest recesses of my soul. I focused on taking care of myself and Millie and for the first time in years, I stopped looking outside for happiness and was content to be on my own. I actually remember the heaviness shifting from my heart when I closed my door at night and thanked God the relationship with Paul was over. I felt this overwhelming sense of peace and love because I'd had the courage to walk away. For the first time in years, I was actually happy – genuinely hand-on-heart happy. And this happiness was met in the most poetic of ways. It was only when I stopped searching for love outside of myself and started feeding the love within me, that the door opened and a new man walked in. It turned out that the universe hadn't given up on me. Just two months after Paul walked out of my life, Tony, my beloved husband, walked in.

"Someone I once loved gave me a box full of darkness.
It took me years to understand that this, too, was a gift"

– Mary Oliver

I met Tony Delaney on Saturday 14th September 2002 at The Pines Hotel in Luton. We were introduced by mutual friends who were keen to do some matchmaking and had an inkling that we would be perfect together. I was so relieved to have been released from my relationship with Paul and happy to be living on my own again with my little girl, that the last thing I cared about was letting someone else into my life. Of course, all that changed when Tony Delaney walked into the bar. I can honestly say that it was love at first sight. Tony was wearing cream cords, a brown linen shirt and his hair was speckled grey. He was 6ft2, handsome, Irish and nervous. He walked with his head down and his right fist clenched. I could feel his energy straight away. If I close my eyes and go into my heart, I can still summon him up. It's as if he walked through that door only yesterday. That is the ultimate blessing of the love we shared.

We had some drinks and went on to a Chinese restaurant, where I spent the evening poking him with chopsticks, which he complained was mildly annoying, but that didn't stop him from sneaking a kiss in the back of the taxi on the way home. He came back to my house and we stayed up all night talking and sharing stories about our pasts. It seemed like we had travelled a similar path and by the morning I pretty much knew that I wanted to spend the rest of my life with this man. Tony knew it instantly too, and although he was unattached, he did have a loose thing going on with a girl whom I called 'the Kiwi'. She was from New Zealand, and I never did find out her real name. He was meeting her later that day to see The Lion King on stage in London – it was his favourite show and he'd seen it four times already. I made a point of telling him that he could only have my number if he dumped 'the Kiwi'. We laughed about it, but I remember him looking me in the eye and saying, very sincerely, "Dee, I'm not one for playing games, so yes, I would love your number." And boy did I make sure he had it. I gave him a small piece of paper containing my home number, my work number, my mobile number and my email address – he took the paper and laughed when he saw the list of contacts. There was no way I was letting him get away.

"I guess I have no excuses then," he said.

After that day we were pretty much inseparable. He dumped 'the Kiwi', came round every night for three weeks straight and had moved in by January 2003. We were engaged by May and we married the following year, on 26th August 2004. Tony was my husband, my friend, my soul mate, my everything.

We danced the dance of married life with mutual respect for one another and flowed with the ups and downs that came from building a partnership and balancing the egos of two quite different people. Tony was a gentle soul. Mild-mannered and cautious, he valued the simple pleasures in life, such as watching his beloved Fulham FC play on Saturday afternoon, catching up with the lads for a pint on Friday night and spending Sunday lunch with his family, which he did most weeks. He was a good, dutiful son, and I admired the close bond that he shared with his family, especially his mother who kept a tight ship and was adored by everyone. Tony wasn't particularly interested in climbing the corporate ladder, but he progressed up the ranks anyway. His success came naturally, as he was super-efficient and very likeable. His biggest extravagance was travel, and in the first few years of our marriage, when there was an abundance of money and time, we enjoyed lots of weekends away, mainly in Ireland, which was Tony's 'happy' place. I believe that we all have a happy place; somewhere where our spirit becomes alive and we glow with happiness that radiates from every cell in our body. My happy place is India, but Tony's was much closer to home. He loved the smell of the peat in the country air, the food (he could eat three bags of Tayto cheese and onion crisps in one go) and, of course, he loved his pint of Guinness. He'd spent every summer of his childhood with his cousins at Granny McNicholas's in County Mayo in the West of Ireland, and he talked fondly of those times. He was always melancholy when we left, and he held onto the dream of living back 'home' one day.

Aside from his melancholy when our holidays came to an end, there was also a deep, more permanent sadness within Tony. His son Nicholas was born out of wedlock when he was just 20, much to the disappointment of his parents who held very traditional views of marriage and family, and it took them a while to accept the situation, which caused him great pain. The relationship with Nicholas' mum fizzled out and they separated after two years. She remarried and took their son to Newcastle, which is a five-hour drive from London. Tony had a bitter fight on his hands to see his son, a fight that ate into his spirit and lasted for years. Tony wasn't a very open man; he was stubborn and tended to internalise his emotions. If he couldn't see a way around a problem he would just shut down. One ex-girlfriend used to call him the 'emotional refrigerator' because he just wasn't prepared to have those difficult conversations that we all need to have sometimes in life. When we argued, Tony could lock me out for days. He would ignore me, give me the cold shoulder and he rarely apologised first. It was his way, but it wasn't mine. I'm the complete opposite – I'm chatty and very open. I need to express myself and resolve a dispute quickly, with lots of talking and compromise. I believe our emotions have to be released otherwise they manifest into some form of pain or disease inside the body. But Tony held onto his pain, and I suspect all those years spent fighting to see his son left a deep scar on his heart, that beautiful, kind heart, which eventually gave up holding on.

As for me, what was I like back then? Well, I was pretty much the complete opposite of Tony. Where he was grounded, I was flighty, where he was a conformist, I was a maverick, where he was cautious, I was a risk-taker, where he was practical, I was a dreamer, and where he was laidback, I ran on ambition. But for all our differences, we made it work. We had a foundation so strong in a love that we were both so grateful to find, and we had a shared passion for travel and socialising. These similarities far outweighed the differences in our approach to life.

We both loved to entertain, that's the Irish in us, and we regularly hosted parties at our house. Tony loved nothing more than to drink into the small hours and sing along with his booming pub voice to '80s classics. Music was his second passion in life, after Fulham FC, and Bruce Springsteen was his God. When Bruce went on tour, Tony would usually go to see his gig at least four times. He travelled all over the world to see The Boss, and when we got engaged, I took him to see Bruce in New York. At seven months pregnant, my birthday present was to stand in the mosh pit at Wembley watching Bruce in concert again. I was a very accommodating wife and I didn't mind, well, not really! And I called in my one and only favour from my time working at the BBC to get Tony into an intimate concert in which Bruce played in front of just 300 guests at St Luke's Church in London. When he got to the door and realised he was on the guestlist, he phoned to thank me and cried his eyes out. I had just made a little boy's dream come true. So, it almost goes without saying that music was a big part of Tony's life. He had a legendary vinyl and CD collection and he loved to spend hours making playlists for our parties. His music collection and Fulham programmes were his prized possessions. I bought him his precious iPod and a Bose docking station as a Christmas present the year we first met in 2002, and he was amazed at the little piece of technology that allowed him to carry his vast music collection around in his back pocket. He spent hours uploading his entire catalogue onto the player and arranging songs into amazing playlists for all our parties.

Our friends saw us as a beautiful power couple. We were two people who had found each other after a rocky start in life. We had an enviable lifestyle, fantastic careers and a beautiful home. To the outside world, we had it all, but it wasn't enough for me. I wanted the family I had always dreamed of, with a mum, dad and two kids. I wanted another child. Initially, Tony wasn't so keen. His experience with Nick and the painful battle to see his son had left a deep scar on his heart, and he was happy with the family he had. He wasn't searching for anything else, but I was. I longed for another child to make my family complete and truth be known, I longed for another child to make me complete. There was something very primal within me that wanted, or rather needed this second child, and if I'm honest I think it was to do with making amends for the child I didn't bring into the world when I was with Paul. But of course, you can't replace one child with another, and when beautiful Fionn came into the world on 7th August 2008, our hearts were filled with joy and I pushed the memory of my lost child into the wound that was buried deep in my heart. I had my dream now: the husband, the family and the house. Life was complete. And Tony embraced fatherhood like no other man. He was inseparable from his little boy. From the moment I pushed Fionn out of my body, Fionn was in his father's arms and I barely got a look in.

We settled into domestic harmony, I took a year's maternity leave and loved being a mum and a housewife, and when I returned to work at the BBC, we did our best to juggle our challenging jobs around childcare and family time. Tony's work frequently took him to Europe, which he didn't particularly enjoy as he preferred to be at home with us. He usually got the last flight home rather than stay over in some faceless corporate hotel, but he made an exception when he got the chance to stay in the Ritz Berlin! I don't think Tony could quite believe he had come that far in life to be staying in such a grand place. He still saw himself as a slightly awkward Irish boy from Southgate, London.

And so, life was good. Tony had just been promoted at work, we had finished rebuilding our beautiful home, his little boy Fionn filled his heart with unimaginable joy, and Fulham FC had got to the Europa League final – the first time in the club's history. And as for our relationship, well, that seemed to be turning a corner. We loved each other dearly but, as with most married couples, we had our ups and downs. I knew he loved me dearly but he had become a bit distant and withdrawn after our son was born. I put it down to the strains of having a new baby, the pressures of work and giving all his energy to renovating our house. We had a lot going on. I tried not to worry, and I prayed that it was just the flow of normal married life and that we would be back riding the crest of the wave again.

The night before Tony headed off to Scotland to start his walk was a run-of-the-mill evening. He returned home from work at 6 pm and we ate dinner together around the kitchen table with my daughter Millie, who was 12 at the time, and our little boy Fionn, who was just 22-months old. I had a glass of wine but Tony never drank at home, he believed that it led people down the slippery road to alcohol dependency, and he watched me with a slightly disapproving eye as I topped up my glass. We let the pressures of the day slowly dissolve away and Tony focused his attention on Fionn, his precious little boy. The bond between father and son was fiercely strong. Tony was very involved in his son's life and when his daddy was around my wee little man didn't want to know me. In some ways, I've always been grateful that I allowed them that space. It was almost as if Tony knew that his time with his beloved son was limited and he wanted to make the most of every moment he had.

After dinner, I ran Fionn's bath and shouted for Tony to bring him upstairs. It was 7 pm, and as I leaned over the banister, I noticed Tony steadying himself on the console table at the bottom of the stairs. He had come over all dizzy and looked a bit greyish. When I expressed my concern, he assured me that he was fine. He was never really one to make a fuss, he just figured he'd got up too quickly and had a head spin. We thought nothing more of it and carried on the bedtime routine, with Tony putting Fionn to bed as he always did. Looking back at it now, I believe I had witnessed the moment my husband's fate was decided. It was the first of many 'signs' I was about to receive to prepare me for what was to come.

With the kids in bed, we settled down to watch some TV. I had another glass of wine and we talked about Tony's forthcoming charity walk. I could tell he was excited, but nervous too. The Three Peaks Challenge is a real test of physical endurance, which involves climbing three of Britain's highest mountains in 24-hours. Tony had suffered from dreadful blisters during his training, which had refused to heal, so he was naturally concerned that his feet might not hold out. I wonder now if that was his only concern. I remember saying to him that he didn't have to do the walk and that I would go in his place. It was no problem if he had to back out, but there was no way that Tony would admit failure – he was too stubborn for that. In hindsight (again), I realise that offering to take his place on the walk was not really a conventional thing to say, but I would have given my life for that man, such was my love for him, and after his death, my suffering was so raw that at times I wished it could have been me in that grave and not him. I don't know whether it was his nervous energy or my subconscious mind propelling me into flight mode, but we ended up having a blistering row that evening and slept in separate rooms for the first time in our six years of marriage. We weren't the arguing types, but on the rare occasion that we did row, it was usually a humdinger. But we'd never before resorted to separate beds; we had an unwritten rule that whatever issues we had with each other we would sort out before bed.

"Take care up those mountains, I'm not ready to lose you just yet."

I sent that text to my husband at 9 pm on Friday 25th June 2010, the night before he headed out to Ben Nevis on his charity walk. It was the last thing I said to him. I have no idea what guided me to use such words as if it was my last chance to say I was sorry about our fight and that I loved him. You see, when you lose someone to a sudden death you look for meaning in that last moment of contact; those final words, that last look, what you were doing, how you felt, and I've since learned that people who are approaching death often retreat in some way as if they are trying to create a protective barrier between themselves and their loved ones. Everything is more poignant when you are robbed of the chance to say goodbye. I don't remember the trigger for the argument, but I do remember Tony saying, "Dee, I hate you when you drink white wine, it changes you." And he was right, alcohol did change me. It turned me into someone whom I didn't like, someone who wasn't true to herself and was less compassionate and quick to judge. But I just wasn't ready to hear that message back then, and over the years since

Tony's death, as I've struggled with my grief and fought hard not to lose myself to drink, his last words have come back to haunt me.

The day Tony left for Scotland was not our best. He was still grumpy and angry with me over our argument the night before. He refused to entertain any conversation or small talk. He went into his shutdown mode but, despite his coldness, I tried to make amends and offered to help him with his last-minute preparations and take him to the station. He refused my offers – he was stubborn to the end – but I'm grateful that I showed him this act of compassion. I know that in some ways I was just being true to myself and wanting to diffuse the unpleasant atmosphere – this was me to the core – but in another way, I feel I was being protected. I can look back on what happened with a clear conscience because I tried to bring us back to peace. I know I would have suffered unbearable regret and guilt had I not opened my heart and offered my help. So, Tony headed off on his adventure and I went to a friend's for coffee. It was a beautiful summer's day and the children played in the garden as the gathering of mums chewed the fat and gossiped about their husbands. I told them all about Tony's trip and our argument. Then I said, "I hope he doesn't go and kill himself up those mountains, he'd be so embarrassed as he's hardly done any training." Those were my actual words, but nobody really paid any attention to my throwaway remark. It wasn't until much later that my friend Elaine reminded me of what I had said as if somehow, I could have known.

At 12 pm on Saturday 26th June 2010, I received a knock at the door. Two policemen were standing there, and at that moment I knew. I knew that Tony was dead. I looked one of the officers in the eye and said, "It's Tony, isn't it?" and he nodded and replied, "Mrs Delaney, please can we come in?" I wouldn't let them in at first, I kept saying, "No, no, you can't come in, no." I didn't want them crossing my threshold with their bad news. I remember thinking that if I didn't let them in then maybe it would all go away, if I could keep it outside then perhaps it wouldn't be real. But there was no way to undo what had happened. Little Fionn was running up the hallway behind me all smiles, and Millie had come downstairs after hearing the door open. I led the two officers into the lounge in stunned silence and one of them opened his little notebook and delivered the facts, "Your husband was pronounced dead this morning at 9 am, after having what appears to be a fatal heart attack," he said. "His body was taken by air ambulance to Stirling Mortuary. Here are the people you need to ring in the Scottish Highlands at the police station. They will be able to give you more details. We are very sorry for your loss, Mrs Delaney. Is there anyone we can call for you?"

I sat in silence for a while. I even offered them a cup of tea and joked that at least Tony had got to have a ride in a helicopter. And then, when the reality eventually penetrated my soul, I screamed that scream, that same guttural, heart-bursting scream that I'd heard Millie make the day I told her that her dad had died. It was a scream that united mother and daughter in pain forever. As she wrapped me in her arms to comfort me, Millie looked me in the eye and said: "Now you truly know, Mummy, now you know." And there was no denying that I knew.

When you're attached to another human being, as I was to Tony, and when that is taken away, it feels like everything is lost. What had gone was my identity, my place in the world, my whole life. I remember registering his death at the council offices and the lovely lady saying to me, "I'm sorry to tell you, Mrs Delaney, but you are no longer allowed to say you are married, you have to declare your status as widowed." And when she said that it felt so desperately cruel, like another loss. *I am no longer married.* I know it seems obvious, but at the time I just wasn't ready to accept that news. I was Tony's wife and now I was being forced to let go of a status that I had fought so hard to find. My journey to him and his journey to me had been a rocky path, but we had found each other and built a life that we both wanted. Now here was someone telling me that I couldn't have it anymore.

Well, screw you! I thought.

On the evening after the police's visit, everyone gathered around: my family, his family, our cousins, and our dearest friends. The shock and pain were unbearable. I remember phoning his poor mother with the news. She was driving and I heard her slam the car to a halt. She was simply inconsolable. Her first words were, "What are we going to do, Dee?" and then, "How on earth am I going to tell Michael?" Tony's father, Michael, had been unwell for many years. My mother-in-law knew that the news would destroy him. We gathered in our grief later that day and went to our church to light candles. I was an active and practising Catholic at the time and needed to be close to my God. Our priest came to the house later that evening with his soft, gentle words of comfort, but in truth, there was very little he could say to ease our pain.

The next day I flew up to Scotland with Tony's mother and brother to bring his body home. My mother, who lives in Ireland, flew over the moment she heard about Tony's death, and she looked after Millie and Fionn. Tony's father, who was unable to travel due to ill health, pleaded with me: "Dee, just bring my boy home, I need to see my boy." His pain was horrendous. In Ireland, it's commonplace to bury the dead the next day – you die one day, you're in the ground the next. There are no endless hoops to jump through or mindless paperwork to fill in when someone dies. Compassion and common sense prevail; you get the body in the ground and worry about the details later. In England, on the other hand, it can take between 7 and 21 days before a body is buried, but because Tony died in Scotland, under a different judicial system, I had to repatriate his body back to the UK first, so I was at the mercy of a whole lot of bureaucracy. I knew from previous conversations with Tony that he was passionately disapproving of the length of time it took to bury the dead in our country. He believed a body should be laid to rest within 24-hours, so in my heart, I wanted to do this final act for him and get his body home and buried as quickly as possible.

Initially, when we arrived at Luton Airport, we were told our flight to Scotland had been cancelled due to technical problems and there were no other direct flights that day to the north of Scotland, where we needed to go. My spirit was broken. I needed to see my husband: to feel him, touch him, smell him. Tony's poor mum was distraught at this news too. She needed to see her boy as much as I needed to see my husband. He was mine, but he was also hers. I understood that. I was a mother too and I knew the bond she had with her son was as strong as the moment she pushed him out of her body. I could feel her pain as much as I could feel my own. I looked at her and said, with a fierce determination, "I will get you to Tony, I promise."

I grabbed the nearest airport assistant and begged her with everything I had to get us three seats to Scotland. And bless that beautiful angel; within the hour she had us on a flight to Glasgow. Once there we hired a car, drove through the mountains and got to the Highlands by Sunday night. As I went to bed that night, I had a strong sense of Tony's spirit with me. I could see this white, cloudy shadow at the foot of the hotel bed. It was the outline of a person, and I knew it was my husband. I watched his presence for hours. I wasn't scared, but equally, I wasn't brave enough to get out of bed and approach him. I talked to him and cried, "Why did you leave me? Why? I don't understand. I loved you, I loved you so much." And there I was laid bare with so many unanswered questions, but with 100% certainty that my husband's energy, his soul, his spirit, whatever it is that makes a human being more than just flesh and bones, had survived death. It was the bit that made Tony alive. My beloved husband was still with me in that hotel room in Inverness.

The next morning, we went to see his body laid out on a slab in the hospital mortuary. The first thing I said was, "That's not my Tony, that's not my husband." And it wasn't. It was just the vehicle that Tony used for his spirit. Tony's body was parked there on the slab, but he had driven off on a new adventure. I soon learnt that he hadn't gone far. In fact, he was at home in St Albans waiting for me. But first, I had to go through his belongings at the morgue, my heart breaking. And there I found a little piece of paper tucked inside his wallet; the same one I had given him with all my contact details when we had first met. He had kept it with him every day as a reminder of that night, it was obvious that it was precious to him. I remember unfolding it, that tiny slip of paper represented the start of our story together, and here I was picking over the pieces from his dead body, with that bit of paper joining us at the beginning and at the end of our story.

We were due to stay another night in Inverness, but I couldn't bear to stay up in Scotland a moment longer, as I knew Tony wasn't there. I remember being in the hotel reception at 2 pm after identifying his body, receiving his belongings and filling in endless forms. The paperwork that follows a person's death is mind-blowing. It's as if we've created things to do to fill the void because sitting in the void of grief is just too painful. I had his backpack on my back. It was the backpack he'd been wearing when he died. It was still stuffed with all his energy bars, drinks, plasters, and everything he thought he'd need to get him through the walk. It must have been a pitiful sight. The backpack swamped my tiny frame as I told the receptionist my story. With tears streaming down my face, I pleaded with her to get us three flights home that evening. There wasn't a dry eye in that hotel reception, but that amazing woman did it, she got us flights home that evening and my focus turned to getting my husband's body back home to St Albans as fast as I could. When the funeral directors told me it could take two weeks to get him back from Scotland I screamed, and I fought with everyone and everything that stood in my way to make it happen quicker. I was on a mission. This was my final act as his wife, and I'd promised his dad I would bring his boy home. I truly believe that when the will is strong enough anything is possible. And I did it. I made the impossible happen and got Tony home in six days. His body was laid in rest in the funeral parlour for a further four days, to give us time to say our farewells. Each morning I would go up with his iPod, plug in his music and sing to him. The mornings were ours, and as I sang to his cold body, stroked his hand, rubbed his hair and willed him back to life, I thought how he had never looked so beautiful. He was at peace – I somehow knew that. After he died, that iPod was like having a piece of Tony with me, and when I listened to the songs on it, I was transported back to the happy times we shared. Each song seemed to be laced with a special memory that captured a moment of our time together. It was incredibly powerful and, in some ways, I felt it was all I had left of him – he felt alive in the music. When I listen to his iPod today, his music always brings a smile to my face, but in those early days after his death, his music helped me release an ocean of tears. In the evenings his family would attend his body. I'd kept my promise and Tony's father got the precious time he so wanted with his son. On the 10th day, we said our final farewells, celebrating Tony's life in the way he would have wanted, at the Irish club in St Albans. We played his music, drank pints of Guinness and laughed and cried all at the same time.

When everyone went back to the comfort of their lives, I stood still and looked into the void and cried. At night, when the stillness came, I watched as Tony's shadow danced around the walls trying to tell me, "Don't cry, Dee, it's all OK. I'm still here."

But I wasn't so open to Spirit in those early days. Understandably, my faith was shattered, and my heart was broken. I didn't know what to believe anymore. Was it really Tony? Why wasn't he in heaven? Why was he here with me? I had so many unanswered questions. Then one morning, Fionn said to me, "Mummy, who is that man who comes to visit me every night?" I asked him what he meant and he said that there was a man by the window watching over him. I was stunned, *my little Fionn could see his dad's spirit too.* I told Fionn that I believed it was his daddy letting him know that he was always there and that he loved him very much. Fionn didn't question it.

Four years later, when my son was six, I asked if he remembered seeing his daddy at night. He replied, "Mummy, I can't remember but it must have been a shadow or a teddy. Maybe it was a ghost. But I know that if it was my father's love, then it is with me forever. His love travels with me wherever I am and never goes. Not just my father's, the love of everyone's family is always there. And sometimes Daddy's love is split for me and you. Mummy, I don't know anything about my daddy other than that he was alive. But I know he was a good man, that he died doing a good thing for charity, and that his love will be with me forever. And I know he will love you forever.

And so here I am now before you: a woman in her late 40s who has had two children, and a third child in Spirit with three different men who are no longer alive.

How can this be you might ask?

I've asked myself the same question time and time again.

All I know is that love is stronger than death,

And in the end, death has led me to where I am now.

Death came to me as one of life's greatest teachers,

Death came to teach me about:

Anger and despair

Longing and lust

Guilt and shame

Death came to pull me apart and put me back together again,

And she also came to teach me about Love.

This is the story of how I came to be me,

The story of how I walked through the darkness to come out the Other Side.

Part 2

A New Life Dawns

Chapter 5

A Grief Laid Bare

— ❖ —

*"Grief is like the ocean, it comes in waves, ebbing and flowing.
Sometimes the water is calm and sometimes it is overwhelming. All
we can do is learn to swim."* - Vicki Harrison

Grief is raw and unforgiving. It's ugly, indiscriminate, you never know when it's going to hit you and it feels like it will never go away. Well, that was my experience anyway, and I lived in the darkness of grief for five long years after Tony died. It was a lonely, miserable place to be.

In that first year after his death, I did everything to keep Tony alive. I just wasn't ready to let go. Life became one long round of ticking off events in his memory. There was his birthday, our anniversary, the annual summer party at our house. Every day, every week and every month there seemed to be some event or occasion that had a significance that didn't exist before Tony died. And as the date approached, I would start to feel the all too familiar surge of sadness consume my soul, forcing me to remember the happy times I had shared with my husband and exposing the enormity of my loss. It was easier in some ways not to remember, to block it all out, to not have to face the pain, but somehow these occasions sucked me back down memory lane and shone a spotlight on the life I'd had, the life I had loved, and the life

I was missing. Grief is such an individual journey yet it goes through stages of acceptance, anger, denial and sorrow. I understood it all. I knew it was a process that I had to go through, but I never expected to feel so overwhelmed and paralysed by fear the whole time. I was literally frightened of everything and withdrew into myself, watching the world go by from the side lines.

Living with fear was utterly awful. It consumed me to the point that I didn't trust myself. Everyday decisions became a challenge and I felt incapable of doing the simplest of tasks. I actually felt removed from the world most of the time. I lived in a fog that separated me from reality. My body was stiff from self-medicating with alcohol, and I hated my existence. I couldn't bear to see families together and was jealous of their happiness. I noticed people looking at me and could sense them thinking, *there goes poor Dee and the kids, it's so sad.* Wherever we went the cloud of grief and our story came with us. I was like the fly in the ointment, spoiling other people's happy occasions with my sadness.

I started to put on the veil of survival about six months in, I turned away from my suffering and became all philosophical about Tony's death, saying things like, "Well, at least he died instantly so he didn't suffer," and, "How honourable to die raising money for charity." I just didn't have the strength to sit with the pain, sadness and loneliness anymore. The only time I allowed myself to be sad was by his graveside. I went every single day for a year. I would spend hours crying my eyes out. I would talk to him and hug his headstone, and at times I lay down on the earth and pleaded with the ground to consume me and drag me into Tony's grave, such was my need to be physically close to him again. I didn't need to hold back my sorrow in the graveyard; it was the perfect stage for my tears. There is no need to put on a brave face when you're walking amongst the dead.

By year two I just wanted to run. I dug my heels in and said, "I'm not doing this anymore, it's too damn difficult." I was so unhappy and ANGRY, really bloody ANGRY. I questioned everything and everyone, failing to understand why I wasn't feeling better, and how I could still feel so heartbroken and wretched. I failed to accept my grief. I needed to observe it and understand that in time, as with all things, it would pass. But instead, my grief turned into a form of self-hatred that had nothing to do with Tony's death but had everything to do with me. I started to drink more than usual and became determined that life was to be lived now. I sold myself a line that I had to go out and meet someone else and have fun; I wanted a shortcut out of this bereavement. I was papering over the cracks, and I just brought more pain and suffering into my world. The first man I dated after Tony died was ravaged by hardened drinking. He was narcissistic, angry, deeply unpleasant and completely unfaithful. I knew from the first moment I met him that he was trouble. The relationship was very toxic and on two separate occasions complete strangers came up to me and said, "What on earth are you doing with that man?" I have no idea who sent these messengers to me, but I believe they were sent as a warning. I was pushing the self-destruct button with heavy drinking, and it was leading someone similar to my door. That's the way the world works, what you pay attention to will grow. My outside world was a reflection of my inner turmoil, and it wasn't pretty.

I've always had a love/hate relationship with alcohol. I grew up in an Irish community surrounded by drink, with a father who was never at home and spent everything we had on booze. In my 20s and 30s, my life was a rollercoaster of working hard and playing hard. I was no different to most of my peers who liked to play, but I also knew that too much alcohol fuelled a lot of my negative behaviour. I remember being warned about the dangers of comfort drinking by a bereavement counsellor, who said it was easy to think that you are dealing with your grief by medicating the pain with alcohol, but grief doesn't work like that. Grief needs to be faced, felt and released – and the only way to do that is to face every dark, miserable emotion head-on. Alcohol doesn't help you deal with your grief; it just gives you a drink problem to add to your worries. And of course, there was the matter of Tony's parting words the night before he died – "Dee, I hate you when you drink white wine, it changes you."

I was starting to see the full significance of those words now. It seemed that the universe was sending me a clear message. I needed to stop drinking and start dealing with my pain.

I soon realised that my relationships were becoming a powerful platform for learning. I dated someone else a year later who was teetotal, but a massive pothead. Different drug, same effect. He was completely uninterested in a lasting relationship with anything other than his joint. He dropped me like a sixpence after just two months. We're friends now, and he's in recovery with Narcotics Anonymous. I wish him so much love as he's a good man. He explained that he couldn't handle a relationship because he lived in a paradox of not wanting to be on his own but knowing that his smoking was holding him in a place of loneliness. His addiction kept him trapped in loneliness and I felt so sad for him, but I was also grateful for the lesson he was teaching me. He was showing me that I was no different and that if I didn't bring my drinking into check, I too could easily isolate myself from happiness.

Those first few years without Tony were a very difficult time and I wasn't handling it well, and just when I thought I'd faced up to the worst of it the universe had something else up its sleeve. I was 39 when I conceived my son Fionn, and I loved being pregnant. I was one of those mothers who glowed, and I adored the process of watching my belly expand and feeling this new life growing inside me as I became more in tune with my body and Mother Nature.

Pregnancy was always a time of great peace and connection for me. I had a perfectly normal and healthy pregnancy until I got to 29 weeks and my placenta ruptured and I started bleeding. This happened while I was gardening. As I pulled a weed from a flowerbed, I felt an instant tugging in my stomach. I remember holding my swollen belly and thinking, "Oh no, this isn't good." When I went to the toilet, I noticed there was some spotting of blood in the pan and I called the hospital immediately. I was admitted for five days until the bleeding had subsided. Tony was playing golf in America with his best friend Ray when he got the call to say his wife was in the hospital and to be prepared for the baby to come at any time. Poor Tony was beside himself and travelled for two days and nights to get to my bedside. While I was in the hospital, I don't remember feeling particularly alarmed at any stage. I never suspected that my unborn baby could come to any harm – that just wasn't possible in my perfect world. The doctors gave me steroids to support the baby's lungs in case I delivered early, and I was allowed home with the strict instruction to take it easy. Back in those days, I didn't know what take it easy meant and within a week I was back at work, commuting for two hours a day and working for nine. I felt fit and healthy but my body was telling me otherwise. At 36 weeks, I had my second bleed and was signed off work for complete bed rest. This time I took the doctor's orders more seriously, although it still didn't register that my baby was in any danger. I knew many women who'd had bleeding throughout their pregnancies and had gone on to give birth to perfectly healthy babies.

By the time I got to 40 weeks and was due to give birth to my son, I was put on high alert, strapped to a bed and surrounded by a team of medical professionals, who were all curious to see if I was going to bleed out during labour. It was a far cry from the natural home birth I'd desired. I was induced at 2 pm on 7th August 2008 and fabulous Fionn flew into the world in record time, much to the surprise of everyone, including me! My labour was fast and furious. One minute I was in bed doing conscious breathing and riding the waves of contractions with ease, as Tony rubbed my back and read his *Empire* magazine, the next I was sitting on the toilet as my waters broke. The pan was filled with pints of blood and all hell broke loose. It seemed my ruptured placenta was more severe than first thought, and I was rushed to the delivery suite by the midwives, who screamed, "Don't push, don't push," as they took me up in the lift. The urge to push was so strong that all I could scream back was, "But I need to push, the baby is here!" We arrived in the delivery suite and three pushes later – at 6.36 pm – Fionn took his first breath.

In the end, I was grateful to be in the hospital. After delivering my son, the first thing I said was, "Oh my God, Tony, what's wrong with his eye?"

Fionn's right eye was all squashed up and I sensed in that first moment of seeing him that something was wrong. The midwives assured me that everything was fine and that his eye was probably just full of all the goo from the birth. They cleaned him up and passed him to his daddy as I delivered my broken placenta and prayed that would be the end of it. But again, the nagging little voice inside me knew that it wasn't.

Fionn was a beautiful, angelic-looking baby and was very placid and mild, easy to feed, a good sleeper and generally very chilled. He was and still is very content in his own world. He often stares into the distance, transfixed on whatever is 'out there', and he has a remarkable knowing that amazes me. And this knowing has revealed itself throughout the years in the little chats we have just before bedtime or when he's having a quiet moment in the bath. There's something about Fionn's energy that almost draws you in. His inner strength started to appear early on, when his cerebral palsy first came to light.

When Fionn was about two and a half, I started to become concerned about his physical health. As he approached most of his developmental milestones, I noticed that something wasn't quite right. He used to drag his right leg when he walked, and his core stability was weak which meant he struggled to pull himself up to standing. He was very uninterested in pursuing the usual physical activities of a toddler, such as climbing or cycling or running, and he never wanted to challenge himself, or even try. I put this down to the fact that we started renovating our house when he was nine months, and for the next year the place was basically a building site. As a result, Fionn spent most of his early days in my arms, as it wasn't safe to put him down on the floor. But as he grew older, his lack of physical strength was becoming more noticeable. He clung to me all the time and was very reluctant to try anything new. I wondered whether this was his own way of dealing with his daddy's death – he was just 22 months when Tony died, and, if I'm honest, with my own grief to deal with I barely had the energy to support myself, let alone nurture a toddler. So, I hoped he might just come round in time, but this nagging feeling inside knew that something was not right. I asked my doctor to refer us to a paediatric centre, and we attended countless appointments with healthcare professionals and specialists who couldn't find anything wrong with him and treated me like a neurotic mother who was struggling because her husband had died. I was furious at the system, and tired of battling away when I knew something was wrong.

However, a physiotherapist who had been working with his mobility for over a year could also see something underlying and suggested that Fionn was presenting signs similar to someone with mild cerebral palsy. He had tightness in his lower limbs and was generally very floppy around his core, and he also struggled with his balance. I was completely stunned at the suggestion and went home and collapsed on the floor and cried on my own for hours. I knew something wasn't quite normal, but I just put it down to him reacting in his own little way to the loss of his father. But the enormity of what she was telling me was overwhelming. All I could think was, *First Tony and now my beautiful little boy might have a disability, what sort of godforsaken God could do this to me?* It was just too much to bear. I had never felt so alone. But this was something I had to face on my own because in some ways I felt responsible for my little boy's condition. You see deep down inside I blamed myself for what happened in my pregnancy.

When Fionn was three and a half I took him to Great Ormond Street Hospital in London, where he had an MRI scan to see if he had suffered brain damage at birth. Because he was only a toddler he had to be sedated for the scan, which as any parent who has had to watch their child be sedated knows, is such a heart-churning experience. He struggled a lot in recovery after the procedure and kept screaming at me, "How could you let them do that to me, there is nothing wrong with me?" He's told me that same message many times over the years: "Mum, there is nothing wrong with me." You see, Fionn knows more about life and what it means to be whole and complete than I'll probably ever know, but at the time I was following medical convention and couldn't see life from the pure place where my beautiful son dwells. Fionn knows he's perfect, and he knows he's made in the image and likeness of God. He doesn't need you, me or anyone else telling him that there's something wrong with him, because that's not how he sees himself. He is a very content child in his own world. He often stares into the distance, transfixed on whatever is 'out there', and he has a remarkable knowing that amazes me. A knowing that has revealed itself throughout the years in the little chats we have just before bedtime or when he's having a quiet moment in the bath. There's something about Fionn's energy that draws you in as if he's a much older and wiser soul than me, and I have always sensed that he was sent to guide me.

But at the time, the brain scan told something different and showed that Fionn has periventricular leukomalacia (PVL), which is damage to the white matter brain tissue that is responsible for sending the nerve impulses that control motor function. The damage is usually caused by a lack of blood flow to the foetus somewhere between 26 to 34 weeks of gestation. So, there it was. I was looking at a scan of my little boy's brain knowing that my actions that day in the garden caused damage to my son's brain which has left him with diplegic cerebral palsy. For me, this has been one of the hardest things to bear in life, beyond the pain of losing Tony, and it still makes my heart bleed. It feels like such a cruel lesson. Why should my little boy suffer the consequences of my impatience, my ridiculous need for a perfect garden, my stubborn determination to do everything myself – all those things that put me and my baby in harm's way in the garden that day? Why should beautiful little Fionn pay the price for my actions? And, somewhere deep inside, I hated myself for that one stupid act that will affect my son's life forever. It still makes my eyes well up with tears just.

I spent many moments wishing I could make his cerebral palsy go away. I was involved in a daily battle with him to wear the orthotic splints that held his heels down and wrapped around his ankles. He hated them with a passion because they slowed him down, were uncomfortable and made him different to the other kids at school. He gave up on them after two years. Then we moved onto night splints, designed to stretch his lower limbs while he slept. He cried every night as I struggled to get them on, saying they weren't snuggly and he couldn't sleep with them. He used to wake in the middle of the night, rip them off and fling them out of bed – they lasted a year. Then there was the daily physiotherapy which became a battle of wills, with him crying in pain for his daddy and screaming at me, "Daddy, daddy, I want my daddy," and, "Why do you want to hurt me?" The whole process has been exhaustingly tough, and all the while I've had this nagging finger poking me and saying, "You did this to him."

I spent endless days fighting and pushing against everything: his diagnosis, his physio, the constant appointments, but mostly my own pain at having to do it all on my own. It just felt so utterly unfair. And the reason it felt so unfair was that Fionn was a constant reminder of Tony, and the loss I was feeling deep inside. Every time I looked at him it was like looking into my broken heart. As for Fionn, other than the moments when he protested about the physio and wearing his splints, he accepted his body and grew up as a happy, beautiful and peaceful little boy. The fountain of love he has in his heart gives him the strength to be himself. I have never known a child to be so earnest and loving, gentle and kind. He truly is a child of God, and there have been many moments when he has wrapped his arms around me and comforted me in my times of need, just as I did when I was a child and consoled my mum through her sorrows. But I didn't want to be weak and vulnerable around my children. I didn't want to lean on them for support, but sometimes I had to accept that it was all I could do.

As for me, well I know I tried my hardest at the time, but I also accept that I probably held Fionn back by trying to put him in a box that he didn't deserve to be in. By trying to protect him I was holding him down. In those early days as I came to terms with his physicality, I kept making excuses for him, saying, "He can't do this because his legs aren't strong," or, "He can't do that because his balance isn't great." When all along what I needed to do was accept that my little boy is perfect as he is. I've had to dig deep to forgive myself for those early years of lack, where I was weak and couldn't muster up the strength to see beyond his little stiff legs and wobbly belly, and know that everything is possible if we believe in ourselves. My spirit was broken from grief, and Fionn's diagnosis was just another kick in the stomach. What I went through in those three short years, with Martyn's death, Tony's death and Fionn's cerebral palsy had virtually sent me over the edge, and little did I know there was more to come. But there will always be more to come, that's life. I have now learned that it is how we deal with life's ups and downs that makes all the difference. But I also now know deep down in my heart that there is so much to be grateful for. Fionn's cognitive skills are not affected at all, since his cerebral palsy is very mild. He is super smart, reads and writes very well and holds the most amazing conversations. He is emotionally very mature for his age, and he has the capacity to love that expands beyond anything I have ever known.

When he was six, we sat down together for the first time since his diagnosis, to discuss his cerebral palsy. I hugged him and said, "I'm so sorry, Fionn. I'm sorry for saying you can't do things, I'm sorry for not trusting that you know you are OK, and I'm sorry for all the boring physio. I promise I will make it fun from now on, and you have to start believing that you are perfect and can do anything you want."

And my beautiful boy hugged me and said, "It's OK, Mummy, you never knew me."

And then he said, "You never knew how important I was."

I looked at him stunned and he continued: "I have cerebral palsy and that's life. Some people have trouble writing. We all have something. It's OK."

That was the moment I knew the fight with cerebral palsy was over. I was going to embrace it, love it and everything it threw at me because it's not separate from Fionn, it is a part of who he is. And if I'm going to love my son completely, I need to love his stiff legs and wobbly core and little eye squint and open my heart to all his perfectness.

Chapter 6

Getting My Life Back

❖

"When the spell of conditioning is broken, your Being dances like writing on water – spontaneous and untraceable" - Mooji

There seemed to be so much more wrapped up in how I was feeling than just my grief for Tony. His death was greater than my grief, it was the catalyst for change that moulded me into this new being that I am today. In some ways, Tony's death was my new beginning. It shone a spotlight on the dark corners of my life and forced me to ask some soul-searching questions about what it was I wanted for Dee. Everything was put into question and I took it as an opportunity to improve my life from the foundation up. My lasting memorial to Tony would be to be the best I could be in this world, the person I truly wanted to be and to find true happiness.

The process of coming to terms with my life and finding acceptance and peace with my story was, at times, torturous. But with the beauty of hindsight, I now know that Tony's death was the perfect parting gift from a man who adored me as much as I adored him. I have also learnt that this process to heal the self truly has no end. We only ever go deeper into ourselves when we truly learn to be at one with life. As I started to unravel, I began to realise that I had been brushing up against the real me throughout my life. But this being, who dances like water, was hidden behind all the conditioning that we humans pick up along the way. And although this 'being' showed herself many times as I was growing up, I was too blind to see it. It was through my experiences with death that I saw with new eyes. My suffering and pain were like a gateway to a new world, and as I unravelled and put myself back together again, I discovered that there are no quick fixes, no places of perfection to aim for, and no end game. Real life happens in each small moment when we are just being ourselves. Our challenge, should we be willing to accept it, is to learn to let go of the reins and just let life be. But this was a challenge I struggled with for years.

"The ignorant strive to control life. Life reveals itself to the wise."

– Mooji

So, shortly after Tony died, I did what I always do when I'm faced with a crisis and started to read and research ways to deal with grief and heal my broken heart. My logical analytical mind needed to understand the process. I wanted in some way to transfer all responsibility for what was happening to others, to the experts. At the time I believed I had to look outside of myself for answers, that maybe by intellectualising the process I could make the pain go away. It was as much as I could do at the time to stay sane. I had always found Eastern philosophy particularly inspiring, so I read pretty much every enlightening book I could get my hands on, from *The Yoga Sutras of Patanjali* to *The Art of Happiness* by His Holiness the Dalai Lama, to *A Course in Miracles* by the Foundation for Inner Peace, and the New Age Bible *Be Here Now* by Ram Dass. I ensured that all bases, theologies and religions were covered! I also read books on bereavement. I remember this one book called *Living on the Seabed* by Lindsay Nicholson, a woman who lost her husband John to leukaemia at 35 and her elder daughter Ellie to the same disease shortly afterwards. I remember her story so vividly, especially how she described the pain of that time and how it took her eight long years to heal, move on and meet someone new. That fact stabbed me in the heart. Eight years felt like a lifetime to me. I couldn't possibly live in the fog of grief for eight insufferable years – I was too impatient. I knew it was her story, but something nagging inside me knew that it was partly mine, too, and I didn't want it to be. I didn't want to accept my life as it was, but I had started to identify with my victim story: the person who had lost Martyn then Tony, and then Paul. I kept thinking: *What have I done to create this reality? Did I somehow wish these deaths into being?* Lots of dark thoughts festered in my mind, and I was consumed with constant questions. I was sitting with a truth that didn't sit comfortably with me, and the truth regarded my grief. This was how it felt and I had to feel it. I had to ride the waves of grief, feel the tide ebb and flow, feel the pain and suffering, feel the calmness and rawness, to come out the other end. There was no shortcut.

> *"Each of us within us an unacknowledged greatness that is waiting to be found. It is only when we risk reaching too far, that we realise how far we can go."*

I made a few small breakthroughs, during those early years after Tony's death. But the truth is I was searching for answers outside myself, and although the books helped at times, nothing was really sticking, and I was still feeling utterly lost. When I looked in the mirror, I just didn't recognise the person in front of me. My body was holding onto so much pain and felt heavy and stiff, like I was carrying the weight of the world inside of me. I didn't know how to relax, and the warrior in me was slaying demons inside as a result of all the spiritual navel gazing. There was no vitality or joy in my eyes, my skin was grey and lifeless, and I felt like the darkness was eating away at my soul. I had lost all sense of SELF, and it was clear to me that I had to do something radical to shift out of this stinky soup that was consuming my every waking moment. It was heart-breaking to realise the extent to which I had abandoned myself in life. I had attached all my value and identity on my status, to being a wife, mother, daughter, friend and media guru, but these labels were things I did, functions I performed, roles I played, they weren't really who I was. All the spiritual books, and 'mind' stuff, just left me being more self-critical, at a time when I really needed to feel more deeply, not think more intensely. I thought I was empowering myself, but I only became more confused, and still had no idea who I *was*. As I morphed into this new spiritualised version of myself, I was undoubtedly influenced by the beliefs and opinions that I read in these books. And whilst I found them comforting and helpful at the time, I discovered later, that this was a stage in the process that I needed to go through, until I could trust myself enough to find my own truth, inside of me.

After spending a lifetime giving my power away, playing other people's games, it was now time for me to take control of my life and discover what it is that I wanted for me. I was done with the bull shit labels, with people pleasing and conforming to the will of others. And I was definitely done with being the good girl. It was time for me to step up, to stop being so afraid, and give myself the gift of fearlessly fighting for me. Death had unravelled me to the core, and now it was time to put myself back together, and move forward in life. And the only way I was going to do that was by re-discovering me. Who Am I? What makes me tick ? What do I want in life? These where nagging questions that I had to ask myself, and to get the answers I had to put myself in the centre of my universe for the first. I had to break down a lot of my own value judgements about what was important in life, and I had to stop identifying with my story; be it my widow story, or my career story, because I had become lost in the story. I was mindful that I only ever showed up for myself as little pieces of who I am. I compartmentalised my world, and never truly experienced life wholly and completely in the fullness of my being. I wanted to find the real me, and this meant I had to reclaim all the little pieces of me, that I had given to the ethers, and put myself back together like an exquisite masterpiece. And that meant

I had to let go of many aspects of my Self to create room for the real Dolores Delaney to step in .

One of the first things to go was my job. I loved my time in the media; it helped fund my very nice middle-class lifestyle and brought me lifelong friends whom I admire and love, but I just couldn't cope with the pressures of juggling a big career, and managing two small children anymore. In many ways it would have been easier to stay hidden behind the veil and just get on with the life I was familiar with, but something deep within me was calling for radical change. And this something inside of me was done with pussy footing around. I also felt a deep sense of obligation like, somehow, I owed it to Tony's memory, to find happiness again . I carried a tremendous burden inside me, some might call it survivors guilt, although it didn't feel like guilt as such, it felt more like responsibility. I put huge pressure on myself to do whatever it took to turn this tragedy into something better. My love for my late husband drove this, and it dragged me screaming and kicking into the dark spaces inside my heart, in search of answers and some semblance of peace. I needed to find a way to cut through all the pain I was holding onto, and the only person who could do it was me . Having the time, space and resources to do this was a huge bonus. Being widowed to an executive at a consulting firm came with a price, and I found myself free of the financial struggles that many other people in my situation faced. My mortgage was paid off through life insurances and I was able to comfortably live off the income that I made from my husband's pensions and his death in service payment which I invested well. I was able to leave my job and fully focus on me, which was the best decision I ever made.

"They deem me mad because I will not sell my days for gold
And I deem them mad because they think my days have a price."

– Kahlil Gibran

So, I took early retirement from my executive job at the BBC in 2011, at the ripe old age of 41, and threw myself into practising and studying yoga. Yoga has, in many ways, been my lifesaver. The embrace of yoga kept me sane when my mind was troubled, and it allowed me to see grace when I felt so desperately sad. I developed a home yoga practice and turned up on my mat six days a week, even when on some days it was the last thing I wanted to do. I somehow knew I just had to show up. I found the physical asanas to be very grounding, and something inside me believed with 100% certainty that yoga was the key to my healing. I always left my mat feeling lighter and more at peace than when I started, and that for me is where the magic is. It's in that feeling of stillness at the end of practice.

It was never my plan to teach yoga, but in November 2012, I ended up graduating from a teacher-training course in London and taught classes in and around St Albans. While I was on my training course, I recalled a dream I had many years earlier, when Tony was still alive. I'm not one of those people who has what I'd call active dreams, where you clearly remember every detail in the morning. I am on the whole a very deep sleeper, but this visualisation/dream/premonition was very real and clear. In my dream, I saw myself coming home from teaching an exercise class in the evening to a man who wasn't Tony. He was making me dinner, gave me a huge hug and was generally taking care of me. I couldn't see what this man looked like, but I knew we were romantically involved. I remember at the time thinking, *well, I have no desire whatsoever to teach exercise classes and who is this man in my house?* But, 10 years later, in 2014, I walked into my boyfriend's house after my evening class teaching at a studio in Bushey and found that he had a big bubble bath waiting for me to jump into. He was also preparing our dinner. I remember telling him about my dream as I was curled up in his arms, and I had to acknowledge that I foresaw this special, shared moment. It was a moment of clarity amongst many that made me start to see the bigger picture. I was beginning to get a sense that I really had no control over my life and that it is pretty much mapped out. It didn't scare me or bother me, but rather I had a deep sense of knowing that fascinated me. There was no denying that all the yoga and energy work was helping to open me up to my inner world, and I was becoming more aware of this deep intuition inside of me, that has always been there.

I gave a lot of myself when I taught yoga. I never once planned a class, I just showed up and gave my heart to whoever was there. I know my students loved my classes and my approach to practice was always deeply spiritual, but I found that teaching drained my energy and left me physically and emotionally depleted. I didn't feel as if I was teaching from a place of internal strength. I knew I needed yoga for me, and I gave myself to teaching because it is in my nature to help others, but there was always this nagging feeling that I was destined to do something else. This nagging feeling was my intuition, my inner guide, my truth calling me, but I had been so distanced from myself for so long that I was unable to feel it. I soon realised that this inner guide is the light that is always there, and it's been guiding me from the beginning. When I stopped and thought about my life it became clear to me that the most meaningful events in recent years were never actually planned – they just seemed to happen. I was starting to awaken. This process of opening to our intuition and inner truth cannot be controlled, rather it happens due to a sudden or gentle surrender to the knowledge that is already there. The truth is that everything we need to know is already inside us, and our intuition reveals this wisdom to us moment by moment when we get out of its way and stop trying to control life. We don't actually have to do anything to unlock the potential that is inside our hearts – the potential we were born with. But we get in its way through our human conditioning and our story. When we break the spell of our conditioning, we start to dance spontaneously in the stream of life, and that's when the magic happens.

"The very air I breathe
is given to me abundantly
the Life Force that makes my heart beat
is an offering to be renewed moment by moment
countless realizations of Truth
are presented in continuous flow
ultimately
I surrender
and accept love's invitation
to boundless life"

– Narayan

In yoga, we talk about this process of surrender as 'letting go'. For years I used to grimace in class when a teacher would say "just let go" because for me that had been the hardest thing to achieve in my practice, and in life. When we let go and soften into a pose, expansion and openness happen in the body and we feel the union of body and soul – we feel the magic. And it's the same in life. When we let go of the outcome and this human desire to control what happens to us, life flows with ease and magical things happen.

Today, my yoga practice remains precious to me, and I'm truly grateful for the blessings it has brought into my life, as it could so easily have gone the other way. Deep down inside, I knew it was either yoga or drink. At times it was both, but doing a headstand with a raging hangover is not to be recommended! Luckily, my passion for yoga helped me stay healthy and sober. You need a clean body to practice yoga, as it's physically demanding, and I noticed that when I had alcohol in my system my muscles were much stiffer and it was harder for me to access postures. But the more I practised yoga, the more my body craved clean foods. I stopped eating meat and followed an alkalising diet of green vegetables and fruits. I also reduced my alcohol intake to a minimum and now I'm healthier than I've ever been. For me, practising yoga has always been about healing the soul rather than getting into those pretzel moves and having a fit body. I never really push myself on the mat, as I like to feel calm and steady, but I'm always amazed when I achieve postures that I previously considered out of my reach. One of these is the Marichyasana D, an impossibly hard, twisty pose, which is described as a gateway posture in Ashtanga yoga because it necessitates broad opening in the shoulders, flexibility in the hips and grounding in the feet. I always avoided trying it because it just seemed hideously hard, which I know doesn't make sense, because how can I ever achieve a posture without practice? But, like most things in life, and yoga does reflect life, these things come to us in divine timing when we are ready. And in March 2015, I was ready. I achieved Marichyasana D when I came to a major crossroads and made a decision that changed my life forever. I chose to finally let go, follow my heart and hand over control to the divine inspiration in me, a higher being that I believe has a plan so vast and beautiful for me that I just have to trust and allow life to unfold, rather than trying to make things happen myself.

I came to this place because I had been trying for five years to fix everyone and everything in my path, but the truth was that it was never someone else that needed to change, it was me. My refusal to see inside my own heart had made me blinkered. It's easy to see the pattern now, with hindsight, but at the time I was living and breathing my painful widow story and bringing suffering to my door. Eventually, I learnt to recognise that the patterns and programmes I saw in other people were the patterns and programmes I needed to heal in myself. I was starting to learn about the cosmic laws of awareness, and how these universal laws really do shape our lives. The Universal Law States that knowledge, that awareness, that all living things, that all life, has within it that vitality, that strength, to gather from itself all things necessary for its growth and its fruition. We actually have everything we need inside ourselves already to create the best lives ever - pure and simple. If we want to live from a place of abundance, love, happiness and prosperity, we have to create this inside ourselves first. And that means cleaning out all the old thoughts, all the challenging beliefs and all the unpleasant memories, to create space for more love and joy to come into our lives. We are constantly sending out signals to the universe and we receive exactly what we are feeling inside. Call it karma, attraction, energy or like for like, what we give we get and what we reap we sow. If your signal sends out love, abundance, happiness and prosperity, you get back love, abundance, happiness and prosperity. I knew and understood that, but my ego and analytical mind had been living in blamesville. In truth, my world was showing me a lot of pain, anger, guilt and sadness, and I knew that deep down it was the pain, anger, guilt and sadness in me that was voicing itself through the actions and behaviours of others. But, as we all know, it's a damn sight easier to turn the glare on others and blame them than to face the truth and accept that we are only ever responsible for ourselves. That's it. Nobody ever does anything to me; there is no 'out there'. There is only our inner world, which we project outwards, and all that we experience in life is a reflection of this inner self. I knew this deep down, and I also knew that I didn't like what I was seeing.

You see, I've spent the past five years stripping away at the meaning of everything, to the point where I believe that there are no coincidences. Therefore, if I manifest my own reality then I have to take responsibility for everything that has happened in my life, and that includes the things I don't like. It has taken a massive leap of faith to get to this truth. If I am ultimately responsible for all the ills in my life, then I must also have the power to correct them. And if the source of my reality comes from within me, then the source of my healing must also come from within. Life is that simple.

"Silence on the outside will lead to silence inside. That is why so many spiritual people observe 'silent time' for establishing contact with the Divine and charging their inner batteries"[5]

So, on 21st March 2015, I stopped. I stopped everything and decided to just be. I gave myself the space to be still and to trust what came with the silence. I stopped teaching yoga and gave myself a year off to just be. I set myself some broad rules of engagement. I wouldn't work, I would develop a consistent meditation practice, I would go with my heart, I would allow feelings to surface, I would look within for guidance and I would keep a journal. But I learnt quickly that you can't really have rules if you are just *being*, so I used them as signposts to bring me back to stillness when I veered off the path, which, of course, I did frequently. My heart knew that the path to my inner voice was through stillness. I kept filling the space with doing, and all the doing wasn't making me happy. I needed to sit with myself and ask the one simple question that I've been avoiding forever, "Dee, are you happy?" Yikes, how often in life do we sit down and ask ourselves this question? Am I happy? Go on, ask yourself the same question right now. Sit in front of a mirror, stare at yourself square in the eyes and ask yourself: Am I happy? Really ask yourself from the heart, it's scary, isn't it? Most of us can't even sit in front of the mirror, let alone ask the question. And if I'm honest, it's one of the hardest things I've ever done, but I was tired of running, and there was something greater than me guiding me to face up to my stuff, and to take a good hard look within. I knew it was just something I had to do. I gave myself a year.

A year to do nothing and live in the flow.

And silence speaks.

When I finally allowed myself to open up and see the truth, I was astounded at what I discovered about myself, my children and my life's purpose.

Part 3

My Healing Begins

SPRING 2015

The 12 months that followed my decision to stop, and just let things be, were the most expansive, magical and challenging of my life.

My soul had been craving a new way of being, and there seemed to be no escape from what life wanted to teach me. I was on a journey of personal discovery and there was no turning back. The only thing I knew for sure was that I was no longer in control.

The start of my journey in Spring 2015 was in some ways the hardest, but then I've often found the start of any project or adventure to be the most challenging time. I knew I wasn't going to be in for an easy ride, and I was scared of what I might find when I stopped and looked deep into my soul. During this period, I reflected on my childhood with such honesty and wholeness that I could see my true self for the first time. What I saw was a little girl who desperately needed to be loved. A wounded child who, through no fault of her own, blocked out the pain and suffering that came from growing up with a father who was a functioning alcoholic and a mother who struggled to deal with the life that had come her way. I realised I coped by trying to make things better for the family and by taking on the role of the 'good' girl. I was Little Lola, the girl with a bright smile who helped Mummy with all the chores and who tried to make everything better. I was the child who put everyone else first. In doing this, I denied my own feelings of sadness, anger and fear. I was the child who observed from the side lines, who never complained for fear of upsetting others and who grew into a woman who became co-dependent on others for approval and love. I built a wall around my heart, suppressed my childhood pain and put a sticking plaster on my suffering, hoping it would all somehow disappear if I kept focusing on the good things in life.

One of the principal teachings in Buddhism is the idea that suffering is part of the human condition, and when we understand the causes of our suffering, we can transcend them, so they no longer affect us in life. Meeting myself with this level of honesty, required real bravery, and it wasn't until that moment in March 2015 when I stopped that I really knew how much pain I was holding onto from my childhood.

Over the years I created a blind spot regarding my negative emotions and chose only to see the good in life. By doing this, I created a world with a false reality. This was a world in which I associated love with pain and replayed the emotions and feelings I'd denied since childhood in my adult relationships. I was in a cycle of deep denial and it was playing out as control: control of others, control of myself and control of life. I had lost myself in the name of helping others and the universe was trying to teach me another way. I was so disconnected from the full spectrum of human emotions that it was as if I had denied a part of me existed. This was my 'shadow side', as the Swiss psychotherapist Carl Jung describes it. It was the part of me I didn't want to see – the negative part that had been causing havoc in my life but was also calling out to be heard.

So, I stopped and I listened. I took those first nervous steps on 21st March 2015 – the sixth anniversary of Martyn, my daughter's father's, death. The date was no coincidence. The universe saw it as an opening for my soul to awaken. It was a time to reflect on my outer life – my relationship with Martyn and the lessons he had taught me. This was springtime when the earth is coming out of darkness and into the light. It's a time that symbolises new beginnings and creative expression and provides an opportunity to access the healing energies of Mother Nature. It was a time for change and during these three months the universe taught me some important lessons:

To move forward in life, we need to understand and forgive the past. When we accept feelings and emotions from our childhood that are buried deep in our unconscious mind, we bring them into the conscious mind and allow them to heal.

We need to accept challenges as part of life. There is no light without darkness and no joy without pain. Life is a balance of opposites and to deny one part is to deny the other.

We are only ever responsible for our own lives. When we take responsibility for our world, the world around us changes. In the words of Mahatma Gandhi, "You must be the change you wish to see in the world."

Life keeps on giving. The universe never gives up on you, even if you keep repeating the same mistake time and time again. The lessons continue to come until the soul finds meaning and evolves. Our free will decides when that lesson is received.

Chapter 7

Accepting What Is

———————————— ❖ ————————————

"Nobody ever told me that grief feels so much like fear. I am not afraid but the sensation is like being afraid. The same fluttering in the stomach, the same restlessness, the yawning."[6]

This is how I felt on that morning in March 2015, when I arrived back home from the school run with heaviness in my heart and an unexplainable sense of trepidation. I knew I was about to go to a place deep inside me that I had been avoiding my whole life. I was grieving, not for my late husband, but for me. As I walked into the living room and glanced around at the trappings of my comfortable middle-class existence, I felt only emptiness inside. None of it mattered. I was sitting in my beautiful home in St Albans, where I'd always dreamed of living, but I was dead inside. I felt nothing, just this vacuum of space that was disconnected from anything real. The stillness was suffocating, but I sat with it anyway, I was done running. I knew I just had to sit out this moment of discomfort, and then the next moment and the one after that. I had to sit in the stillness and accept what came. I focused on my breath. Years of yoga practice had taught me that the breath is the gateway to the inner self, so if I could just get past the panic and anxiety and get through the veil between my internal and external experiences, I knew I would get to the other side, to the realm of the soul. The veil is where the battle of the will happens. It's what holds on to the secrets and hurts and suffering of the past and it's what I needed to pass through to reach the timeless stillness of the light within me.

I held this place of stillness for the briefest of seconds and invited a flood of emotions to the surface, releasing with it a torrent of tears I'd been fighting for years. At first, I tried my hardest to stifle the sobs and push them away. My lifelong habit of denial wanted to spare me the suffering and pain. But somehow, I finally found the strength to give up the fight and surrender. I stopped trying so damn hard to make everything OK. I stopped putting on the veil and for the first time in years, I started to feel. An unexpected avalanche of unstoppable tears rolled freely down my cheeks, saturating my neck and wetting my clothes. Although I had cried a thousand tears for my husband Tony when he'd died, these tears were different. These tears were for me. They were tears for the little girl inside me who I'd denied for so long, and who wanted so desperately to be heard. And, as I closed my eyes, I could see a little girl right in front of me. She had pigtails and a bluntly cut fringe that emphasised a pretty, cherub-like face. She felt so real it was as if I'd travelled back in time and gone into my childhood body. I could see the sadness in my eyes and, as I was drawn in by the image of my childhood self, I held my arms out to cuddle her. But she wasn't 'out there,' she was deep within me.

"Oh my God, it's me, it's me, it's me," I cried. I wanted to cuddle her and tell her everything would be OK. And, as this realisation dawned on me, my arms naturally found their way around my shoulders and I gave myself a loving, nurturing embrace.

"It's OK, little Lola," I whispered. "I am with you now."

The whole experience felt raw and so very painful. It hurt to know I'd denied all these feelings for so many years and had lived behind an impenetrable façade, one that was now showing signs of cracking and allowing the light of truth to shine through. But as I nurtured my child within and told her how much I loved her, I also experienced a beautiful moment of deep healing. And that really was the moment my life changed forever. I made the choice then to stop running and to start healing.

"Whatever inner worlds I choose to explore
or how subtle and etheric my sensations may become
no matter how far over time and space I travel in order to heal
I AM going nowhere, and nothing is coming to me
in this silent celebration of unity"

– Narayan

I started to see how my childhood experience had influenced the behaviours and patterns in my adult life. I started to 'own' my childhood story, not from a position of blame, through pointing the finger at my parents and saying, "You did this to me", but from a place of oneness that saw my mum and dad as two people; two souls on their own journey who were doing the best they could. I stopped judging my parents and turned the lens on me. Judgement is another form of control. When we judge we give advice and opinions, but when we empathise, we listen with an open, knowing heart.

Acceptance is the antithesis of denial and control, but it comes from a place of non-judgement, where you can allow things to be without the need to change them, even if that feels sad, frightening or overwhelming. When I let go of the controls and stopped judging, I began to see my childhood stories through new eyes of awareness. I started to 'parent' my own inner child from a place of love. I would sit in meditation with her each day and conjure up the little girl with pigtails. As I gave her the space to come forward, the love I sent her allowed the pain and suffering that I had held onto for years to rise to the surface to be healed. I realised that through the openness of my heart, I could literally reach the sadness from my childhood that was stored in my body and shine the light of love on it. As I did this, I felt the energy of the stored emotions rise throughout my whole body and dissipate out through my ears. I was letting go. I was transmuting the suffering and pain that I had held onto from my childhood story into love. And if I can do this, so can you. By sitting with myself in silence and going into the pain, I was healing myself and making peace with my story.

When we are young children, most of us think Mummy and Daddy are the perfect female and male archetypes and we believe everything they say, thinking they can do no wrong. And while it is every child's basic right to be loved and nurtured, not every child is fortunate enough to experience this. When a child grows up in an environment where their basic needs aren't met (by one or both parents), they will find other ways to compensate for this 'lost' love. And more often than not, they will believe they did something wrong – because in their eyes Mummy and Daddy are perfect. This is just how it was for me. Instead of seeing my father's failings as his own and expressing this loss through tears, sadness or anger, I turned the finger of blame on myself. I questioned why I wasn't good enough and wondered what I could do to gain his love. I suppressed my feelings and did everything I could to try to fix the situation and make my daddy love me. I became the good girl in the family: the strong one who looked after my mum when she wasn't coping. I cleaned the house and from the age of 14, I even did Dad's business accounts. I did everything possible to try to make things better, but I couldn't control my dad's life. His life was for him and him alone.

"Expectation is the mother of frustration, but acceptance is the mother of peace and joy."[7]

Over time, my relationship with Dad improved. As he became more involved in my life, we developed a special closeness. I stopped judging him for being an absent father and started to accept him for the man he was, faults and all. He cried as he walked me down the aisle when I married Tony and helped me renovate my house in St Albans. He knew how much I wanted to settle down and have a place I could finally call my own and it was his way of saying sorry. He also cheered with pride as he watched me collect my master's degree and he was the first person to come to my side when Tony died, picking me up off the floor and holding me in his arms as I sobbed over the sheer enormity of my loss. My children held a special place in his heart, too. He used to take Millie and me for days out when I was a single mum and hated being on my own. After Tony's death, he came around every Saturday to kick a ball with Fionn. And, although he was still fond of the drink, he also found happiness when he allowed a beautiful soul called Betty into his life. She became his life partner and accepted and loved him just as he was. She gave him a second chance of having the family life that maybe he wanted as a young man, but hadn't been able to accept. I will always be eternally grateful to Betty for the love and compassion she showed my dad. She was by his side for 20 years, right until the end.

Dad left this world on 26th April 2012, surrounded by the loving embrace of Betty and his four children. Being there as he took his final breath was probably one of the most serene experiences of my life. I rested my hands on his feet and felt his life force move up through his body as he took those last few steps home. For a moment I felt as if I was in the presence of God, and I knew in my heart that Dad was finally at peace.

In his book, *On Becoming a Person*, Carl R. Rogers writes about acceptance when he says, *"The curious paradox is that when I accept myself as I am, then I change...we cannot move away from what we are, until we thoroughly accept what we are."*

As we develop in life, we are very much guided by the world we create around us. This world is influenced by many views: our internal view, our family view, our worldview and our cultural view. Our internal view is how we see ourselves – it is the lens of our inner self that tells us we are loved, secure, and wanted. But it is also the inner voice and critic that tells us we are naughty, worthless or lazy. Our sense of self-worth and how we value ourselves is directly related to the feeling of being valued by our parents. The quality of parental care we receive as children is fundamentally important if we are to progress into adulthood with a deep sense of internal love and security. Children who receive constant nurturing and love grow up to be adults who have a deep internal sense of their own value and security. But those who are denied consistent care and nurturing by one or both parents in childhood grow up with a sense of lack. They feel abandoned, fear the future and tend to look outside of themselves for the love that is lacking on the inside. As I reflected on my childhood experience and my life, I could clearly see I was one of those people. I began to realise that my constant search for peace and happiness was to do with the fact I carried deep wounds from my childhood, which I had kept buried for years. And my story showed itself through my body, as it does for everyone. The body is the vehicle for the soul, and each body tells its own story.

Experienced cranial osteopaths can tune into a body and read its story, pinpointing past traumas or blockages carried in the bones, ligaments, fascia and spinal fluid of their clients. They can relay these stories back to their clients without them even opening their mouths! It's fascinating work. The body actually has its own divine intelligence and is always trying to commune with us, but most of the time we are not sensitive or open to our bodies and we ignore the little message that comes from within our cells. Healing is an integrated experience, and we cannot work on the mind, and upgrade our consciousness without upgrading our bodies too. As with most things in life, it's often easier to see these bodily characteristics in others than it is in ourselves. For instance, when we see someone, whose shoulders are up around their ears it kind of indicates that the person is stressed. Or if someone is heavyset, this is often because they are holding onto lots of emotions rather than letting them go. Or, at the opposite end of the scale, someone who is hyperactive and thin might be this way because they have a tendency to live on their nerves.

Learning to become more body aware has been an essential part of my ongoing healing. Our generation might well be progressive in terms of technological advancements and global connectivity, but the truth is we are much less connected to ourselves than our ancestors were. This is because technology has cut us off from the source of true power, which comes from nature and the inner wisdom that lives in every cell and tissue of our body. Practices like yoga and meditation help bring more awareness to the body, as they teach us to direct the breath and mind to the part of the body that is calling for attention. When we learn to listen to bodies, we can tune into innate wisdom that connects us to higher versions of ourselves, and the divine.

It took me about five years of daily yoga practice, to start to awaken my body, and for my body to learn to trust me again. I had abused it so badly with excessive alcohol, drugs, toxic relationships, and horrible negative self-talk. I really treated my body like a trash can in my younger years, and as a result, it had become stiff and rigid and contracted in places. But over the years I've learnt to commune with my body and treat it with a lot more respect. It's been a process of teasing out the tension and creating space for more loving awareness to come in. My body feels lighter as a result and is more sensitive to energy. I have learnt to speak to my body and ask her what she needs from me, which is a really beautiful place to be. For instance, if I feel burdened by responsibilities, I usually get a niggling pain in the back of my right shoulder blade. When this happens, I know it's a call for me to look at a situation and make changes in my life. Once I've implemented this, the pain tends to naturally go away.

I began to notice my childlike body and girlish voice, indicating that my body was stuck in an immature state, and that the woman within me had not yet blossomed. My posture also suggested that I was protecting my heart, my shoulders were rounded, and I was closed in on myself as if to say, "don't come near me". Luckily, my curiosity to learn more led me to an amazing book called *Eastern Body, Western Mind* by Anodea Judith[8]. This taught me about character structures and body types and helped me see how my body was mirroring certain aspects of my life, particularly those that I needed to work on.

In 2015, I was 46 years old and at a crossroads. I was consolidating all the knowledge I had gained from around me: everything I had learnt from my spiritual practice, through therapy, through reading loads of books, and through my new understanding of the psychological and emotional challenges I faced in my childhood. I was starting to integrate it all and this was awakening my heart. And the heart is the gateway to universal consciousness.

"When I see you with an open heart
my heart is opened further
into a unified field
where hate melts into love
and love is oneness
uncreated"

– Narayan

When we experience difficulties during key developmental stages of our life, we develop coping strategies to protect ourselves. In effect, we put on our *armour* and go out to either fight the world or withdraw. This *body armour* is locked into our tissues and reveals itself in our posture and through distinctive characteristics. Bioenergetics, as pioneered by the American psychotherapist, Alexander Lowen, uses the language of the body to heal the problems of the mind. His works prescribe six typical body armours that the individual can identify with:

A: The Creative/Schizoid has a typically tall and lean body shape, and appears to live on their nerves. People with this structure overly intellectualise their existence, and their creativity feeds their right to exist, which was challenged by their mother's lack of bonding in the womb and in early childhood.

B: *The Oral/Lover* typically has hips that sway forward and a sunken chest. They tend to either be very small or very large. Orals want to merge with others and are people pleasers. They can be needy and have addictive personalities. They also fixate on others.

C: *The Masochist/Endurer* is typically thickset around the middle and has a dense, heavy body. They hold everything inside and become stuck in cycles of pleasing and resisting, which develops normally as a result of an over-controlling parent. They live in terrible conflict with themselves because they hold everything inside and fear being exposed to their true feelings.

D: *The Rigid/Achiever* is typically a good looking, athletic and high achieving man who lives in the persona of a perfect world, but is very disconnected from the inner self. This characteristic develops between the ages of four and seven when the parent withdraws from the child and expects them to grow up. In turn, the child's vulnerabilities and weaknesses are not nurtured. This creates issues with commitment and fears around intimacy in adulthood.

E: *The Hysteric* is typically a pear-shaped woman, with a small upper body and large hips and thighs. They are overly emotional and crave attention, and this characteristic develops when the father lacks empathy as the child matures and the expectation for achievement is high.

F: *The Challenger/Defender* typically has broad shoulders, narrow hips and a strong physical presence, with a confidence that masks their insecurities. They have a tendency to attack and defend as a result of their own vulnerabilities, which were seen as a weakness by their parents at a time when they were seeking autonomy. As a result, they must win at all times.

Each character type carries some kind of deficiency or excess somewhere along the chakra system, which is an Eastern philosophical model for life. As we develop, we move through each chakra and expand our state of consciousness. What this means in simple language is that we bring more meaning, compassion and understanding into our existence. As we integrate the individual with the divine wisdom of the universe, we learn to live from a place of true empathy and love. Yoga is one of the key disciplines that helps us to work on the chakra system. There are seven main chakras and these run from the base of the spine to the top of the head. Their function is to receive, process and express life force or energy.

> "Chakras are not physical entities in and of themselves. Like feelings or ideas, they cannot be held like a physical object, yet they have a strong effect upon the body as they express the embodiment of spiritual energy on the physical plane. Chakra patterns are programmed deep in the core of the mind-body interface and have a strong relationship with our physical function."[9]

By looking at the body and examining our habits, we begin to see the patterns we use to deal with stress or trauma. Most people tend to either avoid situations or overcompensate when faced with difficulties. Different character structures appear as a result of our excess or deficient coping strategies throughout key development stages. Take a look at the descriptions above and see which character best describes you and your story. I could easily identify myself and my story with the Oral/Lover body armour. In fact, the description nearly flew off the page and I had one of those enlightening OMG moments, jumping up and down and screaming, that's me, I am textbook Oral.

Oral Characters, like myself, are known as the undernourished child. They suffer from emotional wounds and desperately want to be loved. When they struggle to find this love, they find comfort around food and other oral activities, such as excessive talking, smoking or drinking, and so on. They have difficulty forming boundaries, believe that love will solve everything, feel empty and abandoned and have a deep fear of letting go. Oral characters are deficient in the first chakra, whose Sanskrit name is Muladhara, meaning 'root support'. (I will talk about the development of other chakras throughout the book.) The first chakra supports the basic need for survival, safety, nourishment and physical health. It correlates with the development stages from the womb to 12 months and the concerns of trust, stability, prosperity and good health. It represents our physical reality, our relationship to the body and the world around us. The root chakra connects us to Mother Earth, our physical mother and our ability to mother ourselves and others. In yoga, a balanced first chakra is achieved through grounding via the feet and legs. Grounding refers to the connection between the soul and Mother Nature. When a person is grounded, the soul is centred within the body and the body has a strong connection to the earth, which brings a feeling of strength, vitality and balance. This connection comes from drawing energy up from the earth through the feet and along the spinal cord. When a person isn't grounded, they usually feel anxious, fearful and unprotected by the earth. Throughout all my years of yoga practice, I have always struggled to ground my feet. My heels always want to rise off the mat or my toes seem to grip on for dear life. But, as I explained before, the body never lies, and what we feel and how we present ourselves in a posture is always a reflection of our inner soul. Indeed, it seems my feet have been trying to tell me something for years. They were asking me to draw deeper into my roots and reclaim my childhood.

I started to do this by actively grounding myself in my yoga practice. I brought a new focus to my feet and really concentrated on my foundation in each posture. I also spent a lot more time outside in nature, in the ground. I stood barefoot on the grass in my back garden every day for 10 minutes and visualised roots from my feet travelling deep into Mother Earth and drawing vital energy up into my body. As

I took a deep breath in, I imagined this energy of Mother Earth as a golden orb of light drawing up through my feet and feeding my entire body and I felt myself become strong and expansive. As I breathed out, I pressed my heels firmly down into the grass and released any stress or worries that I was holding onto into the core of the ground. This helped my body become freer and lighter. Other techniques you can try include gardening with bare hands, walking in nature, receiving a massage, taking a shower to wash away any negative thoughts or moisturising your body. Eating root vegetables and heavier foods like pasta can weigh you down and keep your feet firmly on the ground.

"The wound is the place where light enters you."

– Rumi

As I actively started to draw deeper into my childhood story, and my ground, I began to develop a lot more compassion for my mother. I realised how in some ways I was repeating the same story in my intimate relationships as she had with my dad. As I connected more deeply with my mum we started to talk about the past and her life growing up in Southern Ireland. History has a way of repeating itself, and the wounds of our parents and ancestors travel down through the family line. The physical and emotional traits present themselves from one generation to the next, so when we understand our parents' story, we can move from a place of blame to one of empathy, bringing healing and awareness to the physical body and changing the negative patterns and behaviours that affect our lives. If you get a chance, sit down with one or both of your parents, or a close relative from the same generation, and ask them to tell their story. What was life like when they grew up? Did they have money issues? Was there enough food? What bonding and nurturing came from their mother and father? What was their diet like? Did they experience a childhood illness? Were there major traumas in the family, such as deaths or threats to survival, etc.? Everything is connected. What I learnt from talking to Mum was that we shared the same story of loss and abandonment; hers was for her father, and mine was for my dad. Talking to Mum really helped to shine a light on the deep emotional wounds of the soul that I was being called to heal. We are often unaware of these soul wounds, but they come to us through behaviours and repeated patterns that occur in our lives. My ability to constantly attract men just like my dad – men with alcohol issues – was feeding my wound of abandonment. This wound affected my mother, my grandmother and my great-grandmother. It had woven its presence through my ancestral lineage, and the energy of abandonment was feeding its way through my bloodline. I began to appreciate that far from being weak, my mother was actually very strong to stay in a relationship that made her so unhappy. Because when faced with abandonment, the typical reaction is to run away, which is how, up until now, I had dealt with it. I would find every conceivable way to push away whatever it was that triggered the deep-seated feelings of grief, anger, despair and frustration from the depths of my soul, rather than face the issues that lay under the wound. To stay is to go beyond the darkness and into the Shadow Self, which I talk about in the following chapter. To stay is to dare to look into our own darkness and the collective shadow of our ancestors. It is here that we learn the most potent lesson from abandonment, which is the art of polarities, and how we cannot be one without the other. And through it, we come to understand that to have been abandoned means we are capable of abandoning, which is what I had been doing all my life – abandoning mySelf in order to please others. We come to realise there can be no love without grief, no dark without light. And when we get to the roots of our abandonment and start to face ourselves, as I did when I hugged my inner child, we start to unravel and bring understanding, clarity and transformation into every aspect of our lives. And through it all, I have come to have deep gratitude for the woman who gave me the gift of life.

For my mum stayed through the pain and suffering out of love for her children when she could have so easily run. And I now understand that my parents were my greatest teachers, and without them, I wouldn't be who I am today.

Chapter 8

Denying What Is

———————————— ❖ ————————————

"Beware of the posture of pretence of 'helping' others
It may be nothing more than a masked avoidance in facing one's
own misconceptions born of a deluded mind." - Mooji

I believe people come into our lives for a reason, and my first great love affair after Tony died was with The Big Guy[10], who came into my life to teach me about duality and polarity and how to confront the problem of opposites in human nature.

I met The Big Guy in March 2014, after being introduced by a mutual friend. Our physical difference was the first obvious opposite. He's a big, burly giant of a man, standing well over 6ft tall and is heavy set like a big bear, whereas I am 5ft31/2 inches - that extra half-inch makes all the difference! I'm slim and tiny in comparison. My body and voice are almost childlike, which is typical of the Oral character structure I discussed in the previous chapter. The Big Guy, on the other hand, is a classic Masochist/Endurer character[11] structure, with a dense, heavy and muscular body. True to his character type, he has a tendency to hold his emotions in, whereas I am dependent and clingy. The Big Guy was the boyfriend I talked about at the beginning of the book who appeared to me in an apparition when I was teaching yoga. He was the first man I ever connected to on a deep soul level, and our relationship has been so intensely transformational that at times we have both wondered what on earth was going on. We couldn't explain the strength of our connection, other than it felt as if something greater than ourselves was pulling us together. This force was so strong that The Big Guy would sometimes vibrate when I touched him. We were like magnetics. And like magnets, our opposite traits pulled us together while our similar ones pulled us apart. The Big Guy possessed all the traits I failed to see in myself, and I had the ones he failed to acknowledge in himself. For example, where I showed strength he showed vulnerability, where I was disciplined, he was undisciplined, where I was serious, he was great fun, and where I was angry, he was contained. I was living a very one-sided life at the time. My friend Jennifer described me perfectly when she called me the Christmas Fairy. I had my head and heart in the clouds, and I sprinkled peace, love and happiness on the world around me. And when it came to my relationship with The Big Guy, there was a lot of giving and not much receiving. I felt constantly drained, as if he was sucking the life out of me. I literally gave everything to that relationship, but I gave from a place that was lacking. I was half empty and broken inside, and I was lacking the wholeness you need to give to another.

The Big Guy was broken too. Divorced for two years, he was stuck in the past, pining for the lifestyle he had with his glamorous ex-wife. He found it hard to accept the separation from his 8-year-old daughter, who he missed dreadfully and lived for the weekends when she visited and was lost in a fog of depression and drinking when she wasn't around. And I thought I could fix him. You see, for someone like me, someone who has been all about trying to fix others, The Big Guy was my perfect match. He was needy, lonely and sad and I needed someone who was needy, lonely and sad to distract me from my own pain. I needed the distraction of someone else's drama to deflect me away from dealing with my own issues. And The Big Guy was the perfect guise. I remember our initial meeting in a bar in St Albans. When I first set eyes on him,

I felt a stab in the pit of my stomach. This told me, 'This guy is trouble' and I needed to run. It was the red flags of my intuition screaming at me that this wasn't going to be a healthy relationship. But some other 'part of me' was curious and wanted to go on the ride anyway. So, I did. I entered a year-long relationship with The Big Guy that felt like I was travelling through a thousand years of pain, suffering, joy and love all rolled into one. I have never been so consumed, so lost or so obsessed by someone before. At times I felt like I was going insane, and at other times I felt such blissful contentment I thought I had died and gone to heaven. And The Big Guy felt the same. But ours was a love affair involving two people who desperately needed to heal. The Big Guy was lost to alcohol and in denial and I was a co-dependent and in denial. To the outside world, I was a sweet, loving yogi, but inside I was dreadfully unhappy and I didn't understand why. Tony had been dead for four years and I generally felt I had done the work and grieved for him in a full and honest way. I hadn't shied away from my pain, anger or loneliness. I had felt every knock and bump along the path of grief, but my heart was still broken.

So, in the first flushes of this new relationship, I thought I had finally found the happy ever after I had been searching for since Tony's sudden death. Had I learned nothing?

We did have a lot of fun in those early days, The Big Guy wined and dined me, brought me beautiful flowers and expensive gifts and treated me like a queen. I genuinely thought I'd hit the jackpot. There was lots of partying and way too much drinking, which I never questioned even though I knew he had been to rehab. In my naivety and desperate need to escape my loneliness, I chose to ignore the obvious and enjoyed the escapism. In just a few short months we developed a deep bond and mutual respect for each other. The Big Guy became my lover, my confidant and my best friend. I felt like I could open up and tell him everything, and by doing so he got to see the real me. I didn't have to hide behind the mask with him – he got the full, unedited version. He listened to me laugh and cry and he watched me scream with anger and dance around the living room full of joy. He saw it all. And he never once judged me. He sat, listened, comforted and pretty much accepted me just as I was. We used to spend hours talking on the phone in the evenings, filling the emptiness in our hearts with constant chatter. We had a lot to talk about, as we both understood what it was like to grow up in a family with an alcoholic father. Our dads actually knew each other, they used to drink in the same pubs back in the heyday of the '70s and '80s. We suffered the same emotional wounds that came from being a child in a family living with alcoholism, and we both took on the role of protecting our mothers whilst our dads were out drinking. We could see in each other the roots of the pain and hurt we couldn't see in ourselves. The Big Guy's pain manifested in drinking too much while my pain manifested in loving too much. And our relationship brought out these demons in us both. The closer we became, the harder he felt his pain and the more he drank. The more he drank, the more I pushed to love him in a bid to save him from himself. At the time, I truly believed I had found my soulmate. I used to say he was the *other side of my coin*. And later on, I found out he was exactly that. He was the other side of my coin. He showed me the other side of mySelf, but it wasn't the bright shiny side I identified with, it was dark, tarnished and buried deep inside me. There were so many parallels in our lives and we felt very in tune with each other's experiences. Just as our father's paths had crossed when they were younger, so too had ours. The Big Guy actually remembered seeing me when I was younger. My first boyfriend lived in the same village where he grew up and one evening when we were out having dinner, The Big Guy turned to me and said, *"Dee, I saw you in a car with your boyfriend when you were younger. I filled his car up with petrol and looked in to see you sitting there staring out the window. I thought how beautiful you were. And I dreamed about you being my girlfriend."*

He even had a tattoo of a young girl on his arm who looked just like me. This was his vision of a perfect woman. I became convinced she *was* me, and that the universe had finally brought us together. My ego went into overdrive and created a whole story about how we were long lost twin souls destined to be together, and how our union was divinely orchestrated to help us heal. In my fantasy world, I had us married and living in the country with dogs and horses in the fabulous house he had built. We even had a baby together. We travelled the world and had an amazing life. Of course, The Big Guy wasn't drinking or smoking in my fantasy, had lost weight and was eating healthily. And, of course, he was madly in love with me. It sounds laughably naïve, but I actually believed it all, even though the reality of our relationship was far from the princess fairy tale I'd created in my head.

And then, three months in, the bubble burst and he said something that woke me up from my dream. We were having one of our famous Wednesday Wipeouts, where we'd meet with the intention of having a nice quiet dinner and a relaxing evening together, but end up drinking into the early hours of the morning and dancing around the living room to old '80s classics and Elvis songs, which he loved. I convinced myself it was OK. You always drink and party too much at the beginning of a new relationship, right? And he was like a big kid. He just wanted to play and escape his own dream, which in truth was a lot darker than mine. So, there we were sipping wine at his house. He was telling me about the time he worked in television and how he 'lived the life', as he liked to call it. He got up to refill our glasses and as he headed towards the kitchen, he said, "There's never a dull moment." I looked up at him and froze on the spot as those words pierced my soul. It was another red flag from the universe to wake me up. You see, until that day, I had only ever heard those words used by one other person: my dad. He would be propping up the bar, and as he finished one of his famous stories, he'd end the conversation with, *"There's never a dull moment"*. You always knew you'd been entertained by Patsy Fallon when you heard those words – we even printed them on his funeral card. And here I was again faced with another significant message. It was the first of many opportunities I had to take a long, hard look at my relationship with The Big Guy and see it for what it really was, but of course, at the time I didn't take it. I couldn't see that I was in a relationship with a man just like my dad, someone I loved but couldn't fix. I couldn't see that I'd tried to control my dad by being a good girl and I couldn't see that I was trying to control The Big Guy by showering him with love. I couldn't see that The Big Guy was lost to drink, just like my dad, and that he would never be there for me until he dealt with his issues – I had no right to try and change him. And I couldn't see that the universe was trying to teach me a lesson about me, not about The Big Guy or my dad. *Every* experience that comes to us is only ever given to teach us lessons about *ourselves*, not others. And this was a lesson about acceptance and control, a wake-up call for me to take responsibility for my actions and to 'own' the negative parts of me that I could see so easily in The Big Guy. The negative traits that I was quick to judge in him were also hiding out in the *part of me* I didn't want to see. There was a *part of me* in deep denial because I was so focused on the world outside myself and wasn't paying attention to the world inside me. But at the time I couldn't see. So, I turned the lens on The Big Guy, blamed his drinking for pushing me away and exited the relationship. But it wasn't easy. This small, scratchy, niggling persistent voice inside kept saying, *"Who do you think you are, Dee? You're a single mum with two kids. Who will want you? You're lucky to have this man in your life."*

All I could hear was, "You're not worthy, you're not worthy, you're not worthy." My self-esteem was at rock bottom. I felt very damaged by my story, as if somehow, I was a bad girl, as if it was my fault Martyn, Tony and Paul had died. The lack of compassion and love I showed my beautiful Self was shocking. And after just two weeks of being on my own, I had a moment of weakness and let The Big Guy back in. So, we started another three-month merry go round of dating, where he went back to drinking too much and I went back to loving too much.

That was how we rolled. Ours was a magnetic relationship of push/pull, attraction/repulsion, expansion/contraction, where two people muddled along two very different but intertwined paths. We fell into a cycle of broken promises, where I would leave after an explosive argument and then return when he promised that things would get better. He talked a good game and promised everything, but never followed this up with action. Our whole relationship existed on his promise of achieving some unreachable goal in three months. He vowed to get fit and healthy, but it never happened. Then he asked me to give him three months to stop drinking. That definitely didn't happen. Then he needed the time to become financially secure. I bought into the promise and fixated on being with him to find my happiness, as he fixated on his own power, wealth and business to find his. He put all his effort and energy into building his business and working towards his plan for the future and left very little for me. But the more he pushed me away, the more I tried to hook into him to complete myself. He would constantly excuse his behaviour by saying, "I'm not there yet, Dee" and I would scream back, "But there is no there!". But in my own desperate need to be right, I missed how those words were meant for me as much as for him. You see, life only ever exists right here, right now, not in the future or the past. Every vital breath we take, every lesson we learn, unfolds naturally, just as it is supposed to. So, whilst The Big Guy was waiting for his material success to manifest before he could find his peace, I was waiting on him to find mine. And if I'm truly honest with myself, I fell in love with the image of what this man promised. I fell in love with his potential, not the man who stood in front of me just as he was. I was so disconnected from my true feelings I failed to see I was desperately unhappy, and holding onto the dream wasn't helping me. But despite my unhappiness, something very profound happened when I met The Big Guy. Every time I saw something in him I didn't like, be it his drinking, his jealousy or his anger, it made me stop and look deep within myself and question my own behaviour. It was as if he reflected back a *part of me* I couldn't see. When I looked into his eyes it was as if the sadness and pain I saw were my own. I felt I was being drawn to him so I could observe my own suffering. The exchanges between us were so incredibly powerful, like a perfect balance of yin and yang energy, and at the time I didn't recognise myself when I was with him. It was like another person showed up, not sparkly Dee with her fairy dust, but an angry, needy, jealous woman, who I thought wasn't me at all, but, of course, she was. And so, after a year of struggling in a relationship where I felt powerful yet weak, passionate yet destructive and experienced terrible pain yet great love, I finally found the courage to walk away for good. That was March 2015, or Magic March, as I liked to call it, because, as you'll find out later on in the book, it seemed that all roads lead to March.

I spent a year picking over my relationship with The Big Guy and trying to work out what it all meant. I racked my brains about what went wrong until finally my curiosity and need for answers brought me back to therapy again. By June 2016, my fabulous therapist had helped me put together the pieces and make sense of it all. When I told her my childhood story and the history of my romantic relationships, she could relate to what had been happening in my life, because she had been there herself. She understood what it was like to be *co-dependent*, which is the concept of losing oneself in the name of helping others, and is brilliantly explained in the book *Co-dependent No More – How to Stop Controlling Others and Start Caring for Yourself* by Melody Beattie. The author describes how people develop their individual self or *emotional identity* as an extension of the family experience throughout their childhood and into adulthood. If the family view was one where the child was encouraged to be seen and not heard and prevented from expressing their feelings openly, or if their so-called good feelings were rewarded while their bad feelings were punished, then the child becomes *Enmeshed*. Enmeshed children have a false sense of self and develop an outer persona that is at odds with their true self. They can feel everyone else's feelings, but not their own. They learn to hold on, shut down and dissociate from their feelings and they fixate on others. This is what co-dependency is, and it leads to disappointment and feelings of rejection in relationships where a person constantly compromises their needs to feed the desires of another. They become afraid to speak their truth because this might lead to more abandonment, which is the demon to the co-dependent. And this was me all over. Learning about co-dependency has probably been the single most valuable lesson in my life. It has helped me to finally take responsibility for my story, and to take responsibility for my experience with The Big Guy. My issues with co-dependency were just as damaging as his issues with alcohol. A co-dependent is a woman who loves too much, and in the book of the same title, by Robin Norwood[12] explains that denial and control are the two key characteristics of this type of woman.

> "The practice of denial, magnanimously rephrased as 'overlooking his faults' or 'keeping a positive attitude,' conveniently sidesteps the two-to-tango aspect of how his shortcomings allow her to practice her familiar roles. When her drive to control masquerades as 'being helpful' and 'giving encouragement' what is ignored again is her own need for superiority and power implied in this kind of interaction."

That's just the thing with co-dependency, it is very easy to hide behind the person who is the alcoholic, and blame them for what's going wrong in our life. Excessive drinking gave me a viable excuse to say, "Look what you did to me," but in truth, nobody ever does anything to me. I bring on my own suffering. Let's face it, very few people would choose to be in a relationship with an alcoholic. By the nature of their disease, alcoholics are inherently selfish, regularly lie to cover up their deceit and are financially irresponsible. They're not the ideal candidates for a perfect match. You would have thought someone like me, who grew up in a family with alcoholism, would have known better. But the patterns we develop in childhood are deeply entrenched into our psyche and often take years to reveal themselves, as was my experience. My lessons have not come easily to me. I have held on to a lot of denial and stubbornness, and I'm still learning to make peace with myself. Acceptance has been the key to my freedom.

> *"Acceptance is the antithesis of denial and control. It is a willingness to recognise what reality is and to allow that reality to be, without a need to change it. Therein lies a happiness that issues not from manipulating outside conditions or people, but from developing inner peace, even in the face of challenges and difficulties."[13]*

As I started to make peace with myself, my second biggest discovery was learning about the Shadow Self, *the part of me* I couldn't see.

According to Carl Jung[14], the conscious and unconscious mind are organised into different 'selves' or archetypes. Archetypes are models of people, behaviours and personalities that live within us.

The Ego is the most identifiable as it resides in our conscious awareness and is essentially how we relate to the external world through our feelings, thinking and intuition. Jung believed that consciousness is selective and The Ego chooses the most relevant information from the environment, depending on how we've been programmed and conditioned as a child. The rest of the information sinks into the unconscious mind. This may then appear later in the form of dreams or visions.

The Persona is the 'veil'. It is the self that we would like the world to see, and it changes depending on who we're with. It's the side of the self that we show at work, at home or at play. So, I can be a mother, or yogi, or a sex goddess (I wish!). The Persona is often made up of all the positive characteristics that we identify with and want to show to others, such as kindness, love, generosity, compassion, etc., and if we are akin to people-pleasing, The Persona will grow exponentially, but so too will the Shadow Self, which is the 'twin'.

The Shadow is the other side of the coin. It contains all the traits we dislike and don't want to see in ourselves, such as greed, jealousy, anger and fear.

To achieve wholeness as a human being, we need to perceive our experiences in life through a process of opposites. This is because life, in its essence, is made up of opposing forces. Left vs right, good vs bad, light vs dark, yin vs yang. One cannot exist without the other, and vice versa. So, to experience the fullness of life we need to integrate the Persona and the Shadow into our conscious mind. This means being able to accept and explore the shadow side of ourselves. In doing so we create spiritual balance, healing and wholeness. If we deny the Shadow Self, if we do not claim and use it, it will project itself onto others. This means we draw into our lives people who have the qualities *we cannot stand*, as we fail to see that we have them in ourselves. And this is exactly what happened in my experience with The Big Guy.

The part of me I now know of as *the Shadow* took centre stage in our relationship. As I became repulsed by The Big Guy's drinking, arrogance and jealousy, something inside me clicked. I exploded into tyrannical rants of anger and jealousy that seemed to consume me and were totally out of character. I regularly stormed out of restaurants, I criticised and judged and I was bloody vicious in my opinion, to the point where I sounded like some evangelical preacher. When I was with The Big Guy, I often felt like a crazed woman who was out of control and didn't know her mind. Being with him seemed to stir up so much venom and anger inside, and I would sit for hours crying as I tried to make sense of what was happening to me. This extreme reaction came around because I lived behind a façade of denial and was trying to control life.

> "When a person is living behind a front, a façade, his unexpressed
> feelings pile up to some explosion point, and are then apt to be triggered

by some specific incident...The angry flare-up over one annoyance in the relationship may actually be the pent-up or denied feelings resulting from dozens of such situations. But in the context in which it is expressed, it is unreasonable and hence not understood."[15]

My personality was completely polarised. I lived on the edges and only saw the world in terms of black and white. I was stuck in my childhood ways of compartmentalising life into good and bad experiences, and the Shadow was trying to help me integrate these opposite ways of being to bring me back to the middle ground, which is balanced and whole. Repression of the Shadow Self and our negative emotions is one of the main barriers to self-love. And this ultimately is what life taught me through my relationship with The Big Guy. Like me, he was living in a place of darkness and depression caused by his childhood pain. But now I could see my Shadow and she was guiding me out of the darkness towards the light. We can work with the Shadow in many ways, and one of the best is via creative activities, such as writing, painting, dancing or making music. *This is because creation cannot happen without these opposing forces of nature coming together. The polarity creates a force that brings new matter to life. We create by bringing the masculine and feminine aspects of the self together, and this union creates something new.* This is the antithesis of our Shadow, which sabotages creation, and keeps the forces of nature apart. When I started writing a daily journal, I allowed myself the space to download all the stuff I had been holding onto in my Shadow. I allowed myself to spew out all my anger, frustration and bitterness as I ranted onto the page. And it felt good. I also created characters for my Shadow and Persona, and I invited them to play in my stories. My Persona is hippy Dee. She has long, brown flowing locks, a soft cherub face and she wears a floaty white lace dress and a daisy chain in her hair. She smiles sunshine, is fresh-faced and full of joy. Delilah is the other side. She's a kickass peroxide blonde with a short pixie crop. She wears black latex hot pants and a face full of angst. You do not want to mess with Delilah! As I started imagining my characters; what their lives were like, where they lived and who they dated, etc., I started to find pieces of my shattered life, aspects of myself that had been lost in the wilderness through years of repression.

> *"What's the greatest lesson a woman should learn?*
> *that since day one, she's already had everything*
> *she needs within herself, it's the world*
> *that convinced her she did not."*

> – Rupi Kaur

I learnt that the Shadow isn't just one person. There are many facets that make up who we are, and these archetypal energies that make us a man or a woman all have their own Shadow side. And this journey into the shadow was taking me on one hell of a ride. It was taking me into the womb of creation, into my true nature, and I started to realise that she is pretty awesome. The process of unravelling the Shadow will, I suspect, be a lifelong quest since it has taken me many lifetimes to accumulate all the pain and suffering that I carry with me today. And that's OK – I accept it. But for now, I am grateful that I am able to release my control over life and accept the parts of me I have denied for years. I'm being gentle as I walk this path, and bit by bit I'm allowing myself to release the anger, jealousy and sadness that I put into the 'bad' box as a child. I am becoming more comfortable with dealing with these feelings and I'm no longer nervous about expressing them in public. I speak my mind more often, and I'm no longer passive-aggressive. If I'm angry, I'm not afraid to show it. As I start to own these 'negative' feelings, I seem to be attracting fewer negative experiences into my world. I get into fewer confrontations with people and don't feel the need to prove I'm right all the time or to even express an opinion, which is a very welcome experience. The bottom line is, the more I deal with my inner pain and sadness, the more joy I feel in everyday life. There is a wave of inner peace and acceptance that wasn't there before.

As for my relationship with The Big Guy, well, we danced the dance of co-dependency on and off since we had split in March 2015. It took me a further year to finally wean myself off, and cut the deep chords of attachment I had to him. We speak as dear friends now, and we share a love for each other that is eternal, but I no longer feel the pull to want to fix him, because I've learnt to meet him where he is. Of course, there is still that niggling *part of me* that wants to hold onto the story, and the dream, but every time she surfaces, I put her right back into the shadows where she came from.

Chapter 9

Bargaining With MySelf

———————————— ❖ ————————————

"How people treat you is their Karma, how you react is yours."
- Wayne Dyer

As those first three months drew to a close, I can honestly say I have never felt so utterly raw or vulnerable. My whole way of being had been called into question via my relationships with others and my childhood experiences. At times I felt like I had been given a good old bitch slapping, but I knew I was growing and evolving through it all, and the truth is, the only way I was ever going to make it out the other side, into a place of peace, was to work through my stuff, with love and compassion for all that had been before. Every step I took was a step closer to home, and as the veil inside my heart started to lift, I began to open up to more wonders in the world around me, and became more sensitive in my body. The energy within me was nourishing and feeding my soul, and it was helping me 'feel' where my wounding was. All the old beliefs, fears and programs of abandonment, rejection, and limitations needed to come to the surface so that I could stand in my power and transform. The more I allowed this energy to flow through me the easier life would become, because in truth genuine connection is ease. It is peace, and I had to start taking responsibility for my behaviour, to grow out of my state of co-dependency into a more mature state of awareness. As I started to unravel, I began to understand myself better, and this gave me the grounding to dive in deeper, on this journey of self-discovery.

The second chakra, Svadhisthana, is about finding peace in opposites, and separating ourselves from the views of others. We cut the umbilical cord to the world 'out there' and create anew from the world inside ourselves. The second chakra is where we learn to receive and express the full spectrum of emotions in a healthy and balanced way. And we get in touch with these emotions through the act of movement. But first we have to allow the past to move out of us, and clear all the old patterns and resistance that is holding us back from our greatness.

> "Movement is the song of the body. Yes, the body has its own song from which the movement of dancing arises spontaneously. This song, if you can listen to it, is beauty."[16]

As the body moves, it responds to the vibration of the 'song' by contracting and expanding. When we are fearful, the body contracts and becomes small, the muscles tighten and we feel stress in our tissues. Contraction of the body usually indicates that a person is stuck in some area of their life. When this happens, the body will feel heavy and exhausted and these trapped feelings will eventually express themselves through ill health. On the other hand, when we are at peace, the body feels expansive. There is an openness and lightness in every cell. Freedom comes from this fluidity. As the life force extends beyond its form, the body feels physically bigger than its human shell. Expansion allows us to access the infinite wisdom of the unconscious mind, where pure love resides. Through expansion, one transcends time and space to join forces with the collective power of the universe from the deep well of truth that all humanity has access to. These moments of expansion come when we are truly connected both to ourselves and the world around us.

It feels euphoric to experience such moments, and in late spring 2015, I had my first glimpse of what it truly meant to be connected. I had just finished a month's sobriety, where for the first time in my life, other than when I was pregnant or nursing my babies, I stepped off the social treadmill that consumed my life and gave myself 30 alcohol-free days to clear my body and mind. I knew it was something I needed to do. I knew that sobriety would help me open up to the feelings that had long become stagnant in my body and were aching to find a way out. And, as I sat in silence with my thoughts each day, I could feel a little piece of me reveal itself. *All I needed to do was sit in silence, observe my thoughts and let whatever was trapped in my body come to the surface. When the feelings opened to the silence there was a moment of acknowledgement – then they were gone.* Years of holding on, of denial, of fear, passed before me in those moments of silence. And as I released the pain and suffering inside, I made space for more love to come in.

At the end of my 30 days, I went out into my garden, to take a moment to acknowledge how far I had come, and to give myself that precious time to celebrate my progress so far. I'll do my best to describe what happened next, but in truth, it's impossible to do justice to the experience as it occurred, because the power lies in the feelings that I felt, and words can never come close to the purity of that moment. I remember it being a beautiful bright spring day, as I stood barefoot in the grass, arms stretched out like an angel, staring up at the clouds as they danced in the sky. I've always been mesmerised by clouds. I feel a lightness and childlike wonder when I look up at the sky and over the years I've learnt to commune and play with the clouds. It's as if they speak to me, and we have our own unique way of understanding each other. As I was playing and giggling away with my ethereal friends in the sky, I felt myself becoming more open as my heart space kept on expanding. When I look up, I am in effect connecting to the higher dimensional aspect of myself which is outside of time and space. As I continued to connect to this beautiful energy all around me, my arms opened wider, my chest pointed upwards and my back arched slightly. It was as if my physical body was exaggerating the energetic openness that was occurring in my field. After a few minutes I felt myself bathed in what appeared to be a pristine light. Everything around me became brighter, sharper, more in focus if you like. The trees looked greener, the grass appeared crisper, the clouds seemed more delicate and fluffy, and the sky looked like a shimmering aquamarine sea of diamonds. As my energy field continued to expand and rise in frequency, I started to see and feel the world around me with a new level of clarity. The best way to describe this experience is, imagine if you will, watching a movie on analogue TV and then watching the same movie in high definition. The movie is the same, but your experience and enjoyment of it, is greatly enhanced by the increase in resolution. Well this is exactly what happens when we increase our frequency, we get to experience the world around us with a lot more joy and radiance. As I stood bathed in the essence of my childlike innocence, I could feel myself in the timelessness of the cosmos. In that moment of pure awareness, I merged with the sky and experienced my connection to the infinite nature of my being for the first time. I was connected to everything, and everything was connected to me, and a feeling of pure bliss emanated from my heart. I was free to be me, and no longer imprisoned by any beliefs, patterns or conditioning. This liberation frees the ground for truth to rise, and creates a ripple effect to dissolve all that we are not. In another moment of pure knowing, I understood that the universe was inside of me, and that my inner world was actually creating my moment to moment experiences . And if I had the power to create my experience, it also meant I had the power to uncreate, change, and heal anything, in this space of timelessness. As I said earlier, it's impossible to describe these feeling in words, but this state of being that I experienced is what I imagine heaven to be like. You see, what I know to be true, is, 'heaven' is not a place we go to when we die, but 'heaven' is a state of being, that we can connect to at any time . And heaven is inside our hearts.

My purpose in sharing this with you now is to show you what truly is possible if you live your life authentically, as you. When I dared to stop and ask myself what it is I truly wanted, I actually started to stand up for myself, and eventually got to create the life that I have today. But it took persistence and effort for me to become the truth of who I am . This process of letting go, and allowing love in, is not a quick fix. As we start to release and unravel parts of ourselves, we get drawn deeper into layers of self that needed healing, and we have to go all the way back to the core of our being. This cycle of observing, revealing and releasing is how I worked through much of my past and healed the wounds of the heart, to find my peace for now. And finding my peace is an ongoing process. As I evolve and change as a person, I'm faced with new challenges that require a fresh level of balance and understanding as I go deeper into myself.

I talk about wanting to find peace rather than happiness because I believe happiness is a temporary emotion. Happiness has a counterbalance in sadness, and both emotions need a place to breathe if one is to live a balanced, wholesome life. When we live from a place that's only focused on happiness, we're being one-dimensional. We live a half-life that misses the fullness of reality. On the other hand, when we live a life that searches for peace, we allow ourselves to accept what is. Peace makes space for the darker times in life, as well as the brighter ones. We find peace by stilling the mind, and bringing this stillness into our everyday lives so that we become the stillness in all that we say and do. All you need to do is sit in silence for a few minutes a day, it genuinely is that simple. You don't have to invest hours in special meditation techniques unless you want to, of course, but every time you find yourself being pulled out of the centre, take 3 deep breaths, still yourself, and drop back in your heart again, and away you go. It is as easy as that. If we find ourselves being triggered, which will happen all the time, the next best thing we can do for ourselves, is to remain calm and not *react* to things that happen around us, rather feel it all. When we react to things that happen, we charge the experience with more of the same thing, so if someone is angry at us, if we react in anger, we just create more of the same. But if we can remain calm and feel the anger as it surfaces, it flows through our system, and out the other side without sticking to us. So many times, our mood changes as a reaction to other people's behaviour, but when we are at peace inside, we don't allow others to switch us on and off like this. We simply feel everything and ride the waves in life, which strengthens and expands our connection to our self, without giving our power away to others. It takes a lot of inner strength to remain calm in all situations, and of course, we all lose our rag at times, but it's something to work towards if you want to cultivate a peaceful life. Another really useful practice is to learn *introspection*. If you sit with yourself at night and take 5 minutes to review your day, it allows you to observe your life, and see where you perhaps made mistakes and could have done better. When we frequently review our life in this way, we tend not to hold on to behaviours that hinder our peace, and we learn to meet ourselves with more compassion, knowing that we have the grace to change at any moment to be the best we can in this world.

So, as Spring drew to a close and I embraced the process of letting go, I became increasingly aware that my outer world was a true reflection of my inner feelings. And the way to bring peace and harmony to my experiences in the world outside was to bring peace and harmony to my inner world. We are all ultimately responsible for creating our reality, and this reality is a mirror of what we truly feel inside. The people and experiences we draw into our lives come to us to teach us lessons so that our souls can evolve in consciousness to a higher realm. The way we experience life is, of course, influenced by our family and our environment, so by nature and nurture, but also by our karma. Karma is the law of cause and effect, or, to quote from the Bible, "You reap what you sow."

Most people come into the world with agreements that often present as themes that run throughout our lives. So, it might be we find ourselves experiencing recurring money problems, or we suffer with addictions, or we struggle to find wholesome relationships. These challenges stir up deep seated emotions like anger, jealousy, sadness, fear etc.... that ultimately point to behavioural patterns that have been affecting us since childhood. When we are in these situations, something deep within us gets triggered. The trigger itself is a gift, because it forces us to act, and we tend to act in one of three ways. We either feed the situation, and add to our problem. Or we suppress the situation, and run from the issue . Both of these actions are avoidance mechanisms. However, life will keep bringing us opportunities to face ourselves, until we are eventually stop running, and start looking within. Every time we avoid an issue the lesson comes back around and drives home a little deeper. Until one day, we actually stop, and see that the same themes keep repeating themselves, and that we are ultimately responsible for these issues, not anyone else. When we become self-realised in this way, our lives change drastically. With this new found awareness, we can learn how to deal with our issues head on. We do this by dropping into the heart, and feeling the love that we have inside for ourselves. When we feel the love inside we can resolve anything. Our hearts open and we receive guidance about what to do. The energy inside that was triggered runs through our bodies, and we realise that we no longer feel the need to react or supress the feeling . As we find the courage to face ourselves and resolve our issues in this way, we start to grow and expand our consciousness, and not only do we become a greater version of ourselves, we also become an example to others to do the same. As we continue to refine our behaviour and beliefs we step into a purified version of self, which is the way nature intended us to be. Put simply, loving kindness and compassion towards our self always reap rewards in this life and beyond, whereas when we act out in anger or jealousy etc. we will always create more of the same. Whatever way you want to look at it, there really is no escaping the fact that we are 100% responsible for ourselves, so we may as well be kind, because we're going to have to deal with our shit eventually, so it may as well be now.

Each person on earth contributes towards the consciousness of humanity, which *in itself* is whole and complete, so every little good thing you do for yourself you do for others too. When life is tough and we're feeling low, never forget that everything has to find balance in the end. As children of nature, we are designed to live by the natural rhythm of the earth. There will always be times where we reflect, turn inwards, and feel low, and there will always be times when we expand, and feel high. Once we understand this, we can enjoy the flow of life a bit more, and learn about our patterns and behaviours through the more challenging times. Remembering that the universe is constantly speaking to us, trying to help us on our way. In fact, our lives are designed uniquely for us, by us, but sometimes we just can't see the woods for the trees and we can hinder our own progress, without realising it. But in the end, all we really need to do is follow the signs and enjoy the ride. If you remember one thing from this book, I'd like to suggest this simple mantra below might be helpful. Everything I have ever learnt can be summed up by these few words, which are self-explanatory.

"Be good, do good, keep the faith, have fun."

First, we have to commit to being good in our daily lives. When we achieve this, we tend to want to do good things for ourselves and others, however that looks for us. The more good we do in the world, the easier it is to keep the faith in challenging times. When we find ourselves riding the waves of life with grace and ease, we have learnt to be in the flow, and we no longer have the desire to control reality. When we free ourselves from control, we have less resistance to the unexpected and enjoy the ride more.

Following the signs and 'being' in the flow, is about being on the path of truth, and accepting whatever each day brings with an open heart and with the freedom to receive, observe and react to it all, as it comes. So, what are these 'signs' that the universe gives us, which show us that we are on the right path and making steps forward, rather than getting in our own way and going off on a tangent? Well, the most notable ones are: experiencing synchronistic events, seeing number sequences, hearing a poignant piece of music, seeing feathers, connecting to nature and observing spirit animals.

Synchronistic events happen all the time, and they tend to stop me in my tracks as I feel their significance inside. There's often no logical explanation for these 'meaningful coincidences,' other than they have a special meaning to me. It can sometimes feel like the universe is knocking itself out, to get my attention, as I see messages everywhere. I get a lot of messages through slogans on T- shirts. I can be walking along minding my own business thinking about something, and then I'll look up and my eyes will catch the back of someone's T-shirt, and I'll read a message like, "dream big, or stay focused" and something inside me just knows that the message is actually meant for me – it's very cute. I get lots of communication through car stickers, and number plates, and sometimes when I need a real good old nudge, I get a collision in my car or a flat tyre. I've had 3 minor car collisions in the past 10 years, and they all came at a time when I really needed to wake the fuck up and see what was going on in my life. They forced me to stop and break myself out of the spell I was smothered by. It was as if I were sleepwalking around an issue, and the impact of the collisions, brought the issue into conscious awareness, sending shockwaves through my body as alarm bells go off screaming, "wake up, wake up." It's quite a thing when we are stopped in this abrupt way, and I'm always left reeling for days afterwards, as it's usually shadow stuff at play, and my mind goes into overdrive trying to deal with the aftermath of what I have been avoiding. I tend to get flat tyres whenever I'm feeling stuck in life. The weird thing is I almost sense them coming, I'll look at the tyre and think, hmm, there's something going on here and a few days later, I'll end up stuck somewhere by the side of the road, realising that my instincts were right, and I eventually have to acknowledge that area of my life that I'm not dealing with, it's as if the flat tyre gives me the timeout to think, and an opportunity to reassess whatever situation it is I'm in and to make a change – or not! I always see these events as cosmic timeouts, as I ask myself, "OK Dee, what is it you're not seeing this time."

The most common number sequence I started to see when I first had a spiritual awakening was 11:11. 11:11 carries the message of new beginnings and is basically telling me that whatever energy I am carrying within me, will be experienced in my world without. I could barely go anywhere in 2015, without seeing 11:11 appearing in sight. I would randomly look up from what I was doing and it was there on my digital clock in my car, on my phone, on the timer of my cooker or on a billboard at the side of the road. There just seemed to be no hiding from 11:11. Seeing it reminded me to stop and reflect on whatever it was that was consuming me and to really listen to the silent voice inside for guidance. It reminds me of the ancient Hawaiian teachings of Ho'oponopono, which is the practice of mental cleansing and forgiveness. The teaching speaks to the power of self-forgiveness, and personal responsibility, and says that if you want the world around you to change, you need to change yourself first, only then will the world outside reflect these changes. This philosophy is so beautifully simple and resonates deeply with how I feel about life and the world in general. I do my best to live this way, and it means every experience I see, feel, hear, touch and taste is in some way a projection of an aspect of my inner reality. And if I am to be 100% responsible for the experiences that come into my presence, then I am 100% responsible for resolving them. In order to resolve the actions of the world, I need to go deep inside myself and clean out the negative thoughts and ideas until nothing is left. When nothing is left, the space that is held can be filled with love as I can return my divine blueprint, as nature intended. That love is then transmuted to every situation I enter into. I use the word love, for the unexplainable mystery of the universe. Some call it God/source/ creator/the divine/ or nothing, but for me, the best way that I can relate to life is through this expression of love, which is pure in its essence.

> *"The purpose of life is to be restored back to love, moment to moment. To fulfil this purpose, the individual must acknowledge that he is 100% responsible for creating his life the way it is. He must come to see that it is his thoughts that create his life the way it is moment to moment. The problem is not people, places and situations, but rather the thoughts of them. He must come to appreciate there is no such thing as 'out there'."*
>
> – Dr Ihaleakala Hew Len

Messages come to me through music, and I usually wake up each morning with a song playing inside of me, as I silently sing along. I have always loved music, and feel very connected to the words in song lyrics, which sing to my heart. Music is a universal language that transcends culture and religion, and I truly believe music has the power to unite us all. Whenever I need reassurance and guidance, or if I'm low and need to be lifted up, I turn to Spotify, search for musical inspiration and hit play on one of their discovery mixes, and it's like every song is perfect for me, speaking to my soul. Every time. Without fail. Music helps open my heart and brings me back into my awareness, and gives me the strength to deal with whatever it is that is making me feel sad.

Feathers were a big thing for me while I was grieving, as they helped me feel connected to the world beyond what my eyes could see. Finding little white feathers on the ground really comforted me in the long, lonely days after my husband died. The feathers helped me feel connected to his presence, which I knew was inside of me, though it was hard to feel anything in those early days, through the rawness of grief. But when I saw the feathers, they helped soothe my aching heart and gave me the faith I needed to move beyond the pain.

When we start connecting to the world around us and picking up the signals, it's very normal to turn to Dr Google and ask what it all means, and I was no exception to this rule. I was forever googling the spiritual meaning for....... *fill in the blank*....... black feather, white rabbits, dragonflies, spirit animals, numbers, you name it, the minute I saw something that peaked my inner senses I would run to Google and do a search. It took me many years of living this way, to eventually have enough faith in myself not to turn to others for the answer. You see the key to understanding life, is not to turn to others for the meaning of your life, but to turn to yourselves and trust that you have the answers inside. We all have our own unique ways of interpreting the world, no one will ever interpret your world better than yourself. But if we keep turning to others for answers, we end up disempowering ourselves, and all this does is to perpetuate the search for answers outside of ourselves. Sometimes it can take a long while until we realise what we are doing, it's a process, which took about 7 years of external searching, and lots of bumps along the way, before I finally realised what I was doing and stopped. The search is all part of the journey of expansion, and with every stage of growth, we turn to others to check in, and for guidance. This is normal human nature, and there is nothing wrong with that, but it is always better to pause and try to find the answers within first, and then seek help if you can't find what you are looking for within. When we go within, we always learn and strengthen our field which empowers us and propels us forwards.

Another indicator we experience when they start to awaken to our inner self is an increased sensitivity to the natural world around us and the animal kingdom.

"It is our natural condition to be at one with the earth and universe. The sages of old understood this. When our microcosm, the energies

*we hold at a cellular level, matches the macrocosm, the world outside
our body, there is nothing that we cannot do. We were born to dream
and then through our expanding consciousness to make those dreams
reality."*

As I grew in awareness, my antennae to the magic of the world around
me became more finely tuned. When this happened, the universe
started to reveal itself through the wonder of nature and from the
animals we share this beautiful planet with. When we become sensitive
to our environment, our bodies crave fresh, seasonal food and our
habits and behaviours align with the four seasons. As the soul moves
to the rhythm and grace of the seasons, we move through the full
emotional spectrum of human experience. In spring, we awaken to the
possibilities of new beginnings as we plant the seeds for new projects
and watch the earth spring to life from its wintery slumber. Summer
is a time to party as the days are warmer and longer, and the spirit is
freer and lighter. In the autumn, we take stock in preparation for the
long winter months and show gratitude for the abundance of summer.
As the leaves fall from the trees, we take time to release and let go. In
winter, we hibernate and rest, just as the animals do. It is a time to
quieten the mind, still the soul and reflect on life.

As I moved through the seasons, I found myself beginning to deeply
appreciate the colour and texture of the landscape around me, from
the barren frosty days of winter through to the lush vibrant growth of
spring, the dry dusty haze of summer and the warm mood of autumn.
And, as the light in me grew ever stronger, my vision of the world
around me intensified. I started to notice so much more detail and
vibrancy. The sky became alive and talked to me through the clouds.
The woods at the back of my house where I walked my dog, Yogi,
seemed to feed me with ideas for my writing, and the butterflies and
pigeons became my constant companions. I felt more connected to
myself when I was out in nature, and somehow, I knew Mother Earth

was healing me. I knew it was all connected. The woods breathed so much life and pleasure into my soul and it was where this book came into being; my ideas were born out of every footstep. I used to receive the wood's wisdom and write notes on my phone. I sensed something magical was happening. I remember one day, when I took Yogi for her daily exercise, I saw a bulldozer ripping the heart out of the woods that I cared so much about, a huge area of land was being cleared for what I could only imagine to be more houses. I really felt for the trees, inside my heart, and it brought my attention to the endless destruction that humans continuously do to the earth. As I watched the bulldozers cut down those beautiful trees, I felt as if the ground beneath me was being stolen. These beautiful, wonderous woods and those powerful trees had communicated with me and given me so much inspiration for my writing, and now it was all being taken away. It felt very personal to me, and I cried as I watched the bulldozers go about their thing, and somehow it connected me to another layer of pain that I was holding onto inside. I could feel my separation from Mother Earth and knew it was a sign for me to go deeper and reconcile my own suffering.

This is when I turned to the second chakra, called Svadhisthana in Sanskrit. This means sweetness. And sweetness was something I was all too familiar with, as it was my default nature in relationships. My past boyfriends often described me as being sweet, much to my utter disapproval. I mean, what self-respecting woman wants to be called sweet? I wanted to be seen as cool or quirky or amazing, I did not want to be seen as bloody sweet. But of course, what others could see in me was more often than not a truer reflection than what I could see in myself. At the time, like it or not, I was overly sweet, especially in my romantic relationships. I was full-on sweetness and light bending over backwards to please, putting my partners' needs before mine like the perfect Stepford wife. And this sweetness showed itself in my body in my excessive second chakra, which is located around the region of the lower back, abdomen, hips and genitals. My hips naturally sway forward in their enthusiasm to please others, and this for me was the clue to everything, the piece of the jigsaw that I had been missing for all those years. You see, the second chakra is primarily concerned with a person's emotional identity and sexuality. People with excessive second chakras are needy and fixate on others as a way of compensating for their own lack of emotional attention as a child. They are overly giving and seek attachment to others to feed themselves energetically. They are the classic co-dependents that I talked about in the previous chapter. Their bodies are either small or large and are always very soft, almost sponge-like. They are often hypermobile in their joints. But they are overly emotional and suffer from poor boundaries because the first and third chakras are deficient. This means they are unable to contain their emotions, which end up spilling out into other areas of their life. And this was me. Even though I struggled with this notion of neediness, there was no escaping from the truth. I needed to bring my second chakra into balance, and to do this I had to learn to contain my emotions by strengthening my root so that I could learn to trust myself again. I did this through the work of the first chakra, where I healed my childhood pain. Understanding the chakras and how they related to my psychological development was like opening a doorway to a deeper appreciation of my body. I developed a new level of understanding through my yoga practice as I started to fully appreciate the sheer power of the ancient healing system.

My body finally showed me how my weakness in my Mulahadara (root/first chakra) was related to my childhood story and my pent-up sadness that was crying out to be released. This sadness had been locked away for years and had finally found its way to the surface. Now, every time I step on my mat, I know that when I ground my feet, I'm building a strong base to grow and heal as a person. My body also showed me that my core needed to be strengthened. There was a disconnect between my root and my core, and no matter how hard I tried to engage it in difficult postures, I just seemed to fall over. Then I would give up.

Incidentally, the will is related to the third chakra, Manipura, and a person's wants and desires. I had a profound sense that I was starting to address this as I began to question what it was I wanted in life. And the truth was I just didn't know. I was at a crossroads. I was fighting against the traditions and culture of my past, and everything that life brought me, and I desired to be free and no longer bound by conformity. Everything I believed I wanted, such as marriage, money, status and a great job, had come to me, but there I was in 2015 unsure of it all. I didn't know what I wanted anymore and I felt very compromised. This conflict between heart and mind, ego and self, the duality of opposing ideas was very much the heartland for second chakra healing. This comes from the integration of mind and body, but also from how we bargain with our inner and outer reality. This bargaining happens when the soul awakens and starts to find meaning from experiences in the material realm.

SUMMER 2015

The summer of 2015 was about freedom and growth as I searched for self-love, acceptance and my identity. I began to observe life with a fresh pair of eyes, which were now turned on me, as I questioned what it was I wanted. As I stood staring at myself in front of the mirror one morning, I looked myself square in the eyes and asked: "What do you want, Dee?" There was no answer. The blankness filled the air as I searched for a clue. All I knew was that I no longer wanted what I had. I sensed that I needed to step out of the mould of conventional living, which was bound by materialism, labouring from nine to five to feed the pockets of big corporations and following a system that is fuelled by capitalism and conformity. I needed to create something more meaningful for me. I sensed this deeply, but I didn't know what lay on the other side. I had to take a leap of faith in the knowledge that whatever was there was better than what I had now. It meant closing the door on my old life, which at times was scary. Over the summer, as I watched my cousin get married in the same church I'd tied the knot in 11 years earlier, in 2004, I grieved for everything that I'd lost. I was still very attached to the idea of marriage and the little girl's dream, and I suffered greatly as I fought with the desire to merge with another. The summer of 2015 taught me about the roots of suffering, and the second noble truth of Buddhism, which is that suffering arises from attachment to desires. My need to hold on was hurting me deeply. I was fearful of the blank canvas that lay before me if I closed the door, and I needed to strengthen my will and open my heart by healing the third and fourth chakras. The third chakra is concerned with the process of individuation, which is a willingness to step out of the familiar and expected and confront the challenge of uncertainty.[17] Meanwhile, the fourth chakra is concerned with self-love, healing the wounded heart from grief, and integrating the inner female and male archetypes, which Jung called the anima and animus.[18]

Summer was also about having fun and enjoying the long hazy days of lightness, where the heart opens to all possibilities. There is no shadow and no place to hide from the self as we step out bravely and grow courageously. In summer, we are warmed by the fire of the sun and the fierce determination of the soul. The summer of 2015 blessed me with the following important lessons:

We need to understand our personal value system, and work towards creating more of what we love . Having a clear understanding of what it is we want from our life requires great strength and commitment to self. Once we know what is important to us, we can start to take baby steps towards building the life that we've always dreamed of.

We need to let go of attachment to the outcome. When we know what we want, we need to trust it will come to us through the right action. If we hold on to our desires, we bring fear energy into play and more often than not move further away from our outcome rather than closer to it.

We need an open heart to receive love. A closed heart can take nothing in and feels empty. It's a lonely place to be. The only way to open the heart is to love the self. Loving the self really is the only work that matters.

We need to find our inner guidance. The masculine energies of the world have prevailed for so long that the feminine energy feels hidden. It's time to liberate our inner guidance and bring this soft and nurturing love to heal ourselves and our world.

Chapter 10

Letting Go Of Anger

❖

"'No'
might make them angry.
but
it will make you free

– if no one has ever told you, your freedom is
more important than their anger."[19]

Anger is the ugly side of grief. And I was mostly unaware of my own anger until it surfaced, often in an unexpected rage, leaving me utterly shocked, as I questioned where the hell it had come from. I had so much anger in me and it held itself in my tight shoulders and through my need for control. It left me shaken, raw and vulnerable and my outbursts were mostly misdirected at my children and family. Releasing anger is about reclaiming our right to object to the things that hurt us. It's about being able to stand confident in our power in the knowledge that we will not be punished for objecting to something. It's about the power to say no. Over time, I started to release bit by bit, as I gave myself permission to feel anger and addressed the pains of the past I had held on to so tightly. As I strengthened my fire and will, I had the energy to release and the freedom to say 'no' to pleasing others and 'yes' to pleasing me. And there was no hiding the fire of truth during the summer of 2015, as life showed me the value of letting go and I finally stood my ground and questioned what it was I wanted.

I spent the first three weeks of the summer in Asia, visiting Thailand with the children, seeing the sights of Bangkok and the amazing Golden Palace, and chilling out on the beautiful island of Koh Samui and soaking up the white sands and warm sea air. I loved being in the East and felt more connected to myself there than I did in the Western world. Something inside seemed to come alive when I was on Asian soil and I genuinely found a peace that didn't exist at home. And that trip to Thailand in July 2015 somehow planted a seed of possibility for another way of being. As I left Asia with a heavy heart, I felt a longing to return as soon as possible.

The day after my return, I had to make a very different trip. This time it was to Ireland for my cousin Helen's wedding. Helen is the youngest daughter of my Aunt Betty – my mother's sister. She married Ciaron on 1st August 2015 in Tipperary Town, which is where my family is from in Ireland. They married in St Michael's Church, where Tony and I had become husband and wife 11 years earlier. I knew this was an opportunity to close the door on my marriage and my old life and finally let go. I knew it was going to be difficult to step back into that church and watch Helen and Ciaran pledge their love for each other in front of God, just as Tony and I had done 11 years earlier, but it was something I had to do. I'd only been back to that church once, which was to visit the priest for a blessing a few months after Tony's death. I remember feeling so saddened by God's great betrayal and by the senseless loss and the feeling of injustice that Tony's death had brought. It wasn't just the injustice for him, it was mine too – how could God rob me of my dream, my identity, my future, my life, my everything? After all, I was a good person. I suppose I must have been very angry at the time, but I didn't allow this anger to surface. Instead, it lay dormant in me for years and bubbled away inside. Now my anger was ready to explode. I knew the wedding would open old wounds of longing for the life I once had, but somehow, I knew it was time to move through the pain and release it.

"How lucky I am to have something that makes saying goodbye so hard."

– A.A.Milne

Irish weddings are big events and go on for days. Well, at least they do in my family. Day one is the initial gathering where everyone meets again and catches up on life. Day two is the main event – the wedding itself – where the female guests pull out all the stops on the glamour stakes, and there's usually a competition for who has the best outfit and the biggest hat. And day three is the after-party for those who still have the stamina, where the bride and groom get to really let their hair down. Quite frankly, I was dreading it all and reluctant about going. I wanted to see my beautiful cousin Helen get married and catch up with my extended family because, as families go, we are very close. We all get along really well and we really like each other, which is amazing considering there are about 80 of us. There have been no major fallouts or old rifts hidden in our history – at least not to my knowledge! But I was also anxious about the drinking. You see, I knew I wouldn't be able to tolerate the effects of alcohol on my clean yoga body. Alcohol these days just seems to leave me feeling very low and negative, as if it has some sort of toxic emotional quality to it. If I drink too much a dark mood descends on me and I feel so depressed for days; I figure it's just not worth it. But despite all the physical and emotional effects that alcohol had on my body, back then I didn't always know my limits, and so whenever I was due to attend a big social event, I usually spent a few days beforehand slightly dreading the thought of it, which in hindsight is actually quite sad.

And so, I travelled to Ireland on Friday 31st July under the powerful energetic force of a blue moon. Each calendar month, the earth experiences shifts in lunar energy as the moon changes from the birth of a new moon (usually mid-month) to the death of a full moon (usually at the beginning or end of the month). New moon energy provides a gateway to bring new opportunities into our life, whereas full moon energy provides a gateway to release the old. The blue moon on 31st July 2015 was particularly powerful, as it was the second full moon of the month – the first was on 2nd July. This meant that in July, the moon had travelled through one and a half cycles from full, to new, to full again – all in the same month. This only ever happens on rare occasions, hence the saying 'once in a blue moon'. The moon itself appeared to be much closer to earth and much larger than a regular full moon, which made its energetic effects on the body even more powerful. Blue moons are said to bring us in touch with our emotional and inner selves, and they are recognised as an opportunity to let go of past, outdated beliefs in order to make way for a new path. For me, it was an opportunity to finally walk through the pain of my past life and lock the door on my grief once and for all.

I travelled to Ireland with my cousin Barry, his dad – my uncle Paul – and Millie. Fionn stayed behind with Tony's family, as the younger family members weren't going to be attending the wedding. We arrived at the airport with plenty of time to spare and settled down for some lunch, a glass of wine and a good old catch up. We made a pit stop for a quick drink before boarding the plane, all four of us aware of the time but somehow not paying attention to it. When we arrived at the departure gates, we thought we had 20 minutes to spare and stood in line, or at least in what we thought was our line. Luton has a small but expanding airport and handles many flights, which mainly depart for European destinations. The holding area for our departure to Dublin was Gate 15 and 16, which by design was not big enough to hold the passengers for two flights leaving at the same time, which appeared to be the case. People were queued up everywhere and the area was very congested. As we joined the queue, we asked a lady if this was the line for the Irish flight and she said it was and that she was waiting for the same one. So, we stood there thinking nothing of it, failing to realise that the passengers for our flight were being boarded onto the plane and that we were standing in the wrong queue. Don't ask me how four intelligent people could have all made the same mistake, but that's exactly what happened. My uncle was wandering around and not paying attention, my cousin and Millie were both on their phones and equally distracted, and I was lost in the buzz that came from two glasses of wine combined with jetlag from my flight from Thailand. There was no information on the boards or ground staff milling about, and at no point did it register with any of us that we should actually be on the plane, even though it was due to leave in half an hour. It was as if time had stood still and we were in a vacuum. When I finally snapped out of my trance, I looked at the time on my phone and it suddenly registered we had missed our flight. We pushed our way to the front of the queue and watched as our plane taxied off to the runway without us. I was gobsmacked. In all my years of flying, I had never once missed a plane, but here we were grounded as our flight left without us. We went back to the ticket desk to discover there were no seats available on any flights to Ireland that day, and the airline only had two seats available the next morning. Shit. My cousin's wedding was in less than 24-hours and we had to get out to Ireland come what may. In that moment of crisis, the four of us dissolved back to our true nature. I immediately went into philosophical fixer mode, taking control and charging off on my white horse to rescue us all, while my cousin was calm and searched the internet for solutions. My uncle went off for a smoke. Meanwhile, Millie sprung onto social media to let everyone know of the impending drama. After an hour of internet searching, we came up with the best solution, which was for me to drive five hours to Wales, catch the overnight ferry to Dublin – another four hours – and then drive to southern Ireland – a further two hours. All being well we would arrive at our destination by 10 am the next morning. And that was that. A simple one-hour flight being missed had turned into a mammoth road trip, and so much more.

It took another hour or so to get my car back from the car park, and at 3:30 pm we headed out of Luton Airport and up the M1 motorway under the steam of our blue moon. I prayed all the way for an easy ride because Friday afternoons on the M1 motorway are notoriously bad and we didn't have the luxury of time on our side. We had a wedding to attend in 22-hours and counting. But my prayers were answered. The traffic was kind, and as I drove up the motorway, we listened to amazing music on BBC Radio 1, which was playing all the classics from top DJs in Ibiza. We laughed, chatted and actually enjoyed our road trip. It was an opportunity to bond, mother and daughter, father and son, but it was also an opportunity to lead by example. I wanted to show my daughter that everything is possible if we choose to see the blessings in what is. The journey could have so easily been one involving self-blame and frustration, but instead, we made it fun. But I also knew that however detached I appeared from any self-recrimination; the universe had given me another lesson in drinking. Let's be clear, one of the factors that made us miss the flight was having that cheeky pit stop at the bar. This threw my senses and made me less focused than normal. It's my truth and I accept that, not with blame, but with appreciation that I am learning my lessons. I'm accepting these lessons and making the changes necessary so that they don't happen again – this is the path to a peaceful life.

We made it to the wedding location exhausted, but with a few hours to spare to freshen up and grab some food. The ceremony itself was very difficult for me. When my beautiful cousin walked down the aisle, I was transported back in time to my own wedding day, to August 2004. As I closed my eyes, I relived that special moment all over again as my heart exploded with waves of longing and sadness. I could see myself gliding down the aisle to meet my beloved at the altar. It was totally surreal, like I was caught in an altered state of reality. I was shocked and overwhelmed by the intensity of my feelings. Every time I thought I had dealt with my grief, the waves of loss, love and passion clawed at my heart in the most unexpected way. I tried to stifle my tears and keep my composure – this was my cousin's special day, after all, it wasn't about me – but when Tony's name was mentioned in the Prayers of the Faithful, as is the tradition in Irish weddings, I couldn't hold onto my emotions anymore. My heart broke and I cried my eyes out. My mum reached out to comfort me, but I pulled away and whispered to her, "No, please let me be." I no longer wanted to hold onto the tears. I wanted to sit with the sorrow knowing that I was finally giving it space to pass. It was desperately hard to watch two people as in love as Tony and I had been starting off their lives together with so much anticipation and passion. Here I was feeling the same sense of love that I felt on my own wedding day, as my soul was transported back in time. It was indescribable. But somehow, I knew it was life's way of telling me that love never dies. Tony's love was still there for me, even though the white wings of death had carried him away. His physical body may have left this earth, but the love I had for my husband lived on in my heart. And it was now time to give that love to me.

The song of love and marriage is perhaps best told through the exquisite poem in *The Prophet* by Kahlil Gibran:

> *"Then Almitra spoke again and said, 'And what of marriage master?'*
> *And he answered, saying:*
> *'You were born together and together you shall be for evermore.*
> *You shall be together when the white wings of death scatter your days.*
> *Aye, you shall be together even in the silent memory of God.*
> *But let there be spaces in your togetherness.*
> *And let the winds of heaven dance between you.*
> *Love one another, but make not a bond of love:*
> *Let it rather be a moving sea between the shores of your souls.*
> *Fill each other's cup but drink not from one cup.*
> *Give one another of your bread but eat not from the same loaf.*

Sing and dance together and be joyous, but let each one of you be alone.
Even as the strings of a lute are alone though they quiver with the same
music.
Give your hearts, but not into each other's keeping.
And stand together yet not too near together:
For the pillars of the temple stand apart,
And the oak tree and the cypress grow not in each other's shadow.'"

The wedding breakfast was long and boozy and everyone dined out on the story about us missing the flight. In a moment of seriousness, I said I thought it was divine intervention and was down to the blue moon's energy. The guests at my table were stunned by this and clearly thought I had gone insane. Lesson to self: it's not easy being a lone voice when it comes to defending spiritual matters, and sometimes it's best to keep my views safely to myself! But I didn't let other people's attempts to ridicule me affect my peace. There was a time when I would have fought fiercely to win an argument, but now I accept that another person's view can't affect my state of being, so it really doesn't matter if my family think I'm slightly nuts – it's what I think that counts.

By 9 pm, I'd hit the wall and had had enough. I felt almost flu-like with exhaustion. I managed to sneak away in the interval after the meal, just before the dancing and real partying began, and went to my room for a nap. I drifted off to sleep and didn't wake again until 4 am, by which point I'd missed the entire party. I wasn't upset or disappointed, as the whole weekend felt very much out of my control. The next morning, I said my farewells and took the long drive home back to England, this time on my own, as Millie, Paul and Barry took the return flight back to Luton. I cried, screamed and shouted into the air as I released the pain of the past and fought with my will to hold on. I was so depressed, angry and plain fed up with life that I knew I had to make some big changes. It was time. So, when I asked myself again what it was that I wanted, I didn't draw a blank. This time, the answer came in the beautiful words of Nayyirah Waheed.[20]

"Eyes that commit
That is what I am looking for"

I wanted to find love again. And I knew the path to love started with me.

***

The third chakra is called Manipura, which means jewelled city. Manipur is a state in North-Eastern India that is famed for its beauty and fine golden silk thread, which is unique to the region. The chakra is located at the solar plexus, around the naval region, and is concerned with generating fire in the body. The fire of the sun feeds the fire of our will and when the third chakra is in balance, the body has vital energy to put true desires into action. Manipura is the powerhouse of our system. Without a strong will, we don't have the fire to manifest and we become stuck in lower-level childlike consciousness. It was clear to me now that my fire needed feeding. My will was depleted and I'd become stuck in time, stuck in my widow story and stuck in St Albans. I was being called to step into my beauty and to stop hiding behind my sorrow. I had sat in the safety of my house in St Albans for too long. I actually felt as if it had wrapped its arms around me and protected me for many years. This was the house that Tony and Dad built for me and it held my heart, but now it was time to release it somehow. I had this sense that if I sold up and moved somewhere new, I could finally move on. So, I put the house up for sale. The trouble was, not one single person showed an interest in buying it. Not one. It was completely baffling. My house is the most beautiful one on my road, it's in the most desirable area of St Albans and it's near the best schools and road links. The estate agents couldn't work out what was going on and neither could I. I left the house on the market for four months and received very little interest, eventually taking the 'for sale' sign down at the end of the summer. It was clear the house didn't want to be sold. It had other plans for me.

> *"A truth which comes to us from without bears ever the stamp of uncertainty. Conviction attaches only to what appears as truth to each of us in our own heart."[21]*

So, I sat with it and listened to my heart. I focused on what I wanted in my daily meditation and kept coming back to this need to have a stronger sense of self. I had to step out of the comfort zone of who I used to be and discover who I was now. And this was the work of the third chakra, and the process of individuation, which, in Jungian psychology, concerns stepping out of the unconscious behaviour that allows us to be defined by others, such as our cultural conditioning and our parental influences, and stepping into our own space. It's about having the strength to say, "This is who I am" and not to be defined by others and where you came from. And that takes strength, courage and fire. For me, this was about cutting attachment to my Catholic faith and stepping further into my truth and my heart. To do this I had to step into my power. It meant taking my son out of the Catholic education system and putting him into a Rudolf Steiner school, where the philosophy is to develop free, morally responsible, integrated individuals. Steiner schools feed the mind, body and soul of the child, and this is what I wanted for Fionn. It was another step out of the system and towards a new life. By leaving my job at the BBC, I'd already turned my back on the corporate world and I'd also made a conscious decision to eat more healthily, and give my body the quality foods it wanted, rather than following any strict eating regime as I had done in the past. I still allowed myself the odd glass of wine, but I cut my alcohol consumption down to weekends only, and while I still had a passion for drinking coffee, I made sure I balanced this with green juice and water. I was committed to my energy work and meditation, and I had planted the seed to live somewhere else that was better suited to my new way of being. I knew I was evolving and growing, but it took vast amounts of courage and energy to stand my ground, especially as I was stepping into the unknown and I felt very depleted and tired all the time. Up to this point in my life, I had pretty much lived a life of compliance, as I'd conformed to the wishes of others and the direction of our family way. Through the work on my first and second chakra, I could now see that my own inner power, my third chakra, was deficient and this resulted in my passive-aggressive behaviour.

Part of the work of healing a deficient third chakra is through exercise and nutrition. Doing the right type of exercise that leaves you feeling energized and full of vitality is an essential ingredient to fuelling the fires of the core. I'm no stranger to this through my yoga practice, but over the years, I have adapted my practice to bring more breath and awareness to my solar plexus, which has helped to strengthen my will. And I've become more mindful about nutrition and moved towards a diet that suits my body – I guess I'm lucky that I love my veggies, salads and fruits; I live on green juice, which I call rocket fuel. I made a conscious effort to drink plenty of water throughout the day, and I really noticed a difference in the quality of my skin and hair as a direct result of doing so. The food game became simple once I let go of everyone else's doctrines and just ate what I loved, and by making my own food more often I began to cook for love, and my food always tasted so much better. To me, food is more about a taste experience than it is a source of fuel.

Being comfortable with expressing anger is also very much the domain of third chakra healing. When anger isn't expressed at the appropriate time it's often redirected towards our nearest and dearest. I came to realise that the anger I directed towards my partners in the past, was very much associated with all the pent-up anger I had towards my father from my childhood. And my daughter got a lot of the backlash that I held onto from my relationship with my mother. *As I mothered my inner child and showed her compassion and forgiveness, my* relationship with my biological mother and daughter started to grow stronger. It was quite phenomenal. As I did the inner work on me, the world outside of me started to change. And I could gauge how I was doing by the feedback from the people around me. I was 'being' the change, and experiencing it first hand through my precious mother and daughter. Our family are the ones who really know us when we face our most epic challenges.

And finally, to heal the third chakra deficiency, you've got to have some sort of direction or intention for what you want to achieve in life. Now, you'd think someone like me who had headed up a planning team at the BBC for over a decade would have had this one licked, but in truth, when Tony died, I stopped making plans. I lost all faith in life for a while and couldn't find any joy in planning anything on my own, or for my future, so I just kind of drifted slowly around for years. Sure, I knew the value of goal setting and visualisation, but there were so many false starts and disappointments, that I stopped dreaming for a while. So rather tentatively, I set out to ask myself what I wanted, and by the end of the summer, there were things I was absolutely certain about. I wanted to be a successful writer, and that meant getting my books out into the world. I wanted to feel peaceful inside, and I wanted to find love. I still hadn't given up the little girl's dream of finding someone special to share my life with. When we work at healing the third chakra, we start the process of opening ourselves up to receive - although I soon discovered we have to let go of the outcome, and keep the faith that everything will, and does, come in divine timing—not Dee Dee's timing!

Chapter 11

Dealing With Depression

❖

"The feeling associated with giving up something loved – or at least something that is part of ourselves and familiar – is depression."[22]

I needed to ride through the waves of depression once and for all to release my heart from the grip of grief and open it to the possibility of love. I was fed up with spending night after night on my own. I wanted someone beautiful to lay their head on my pillow and kiss me goodnight. I wanted to wake up in their arms in the morning knowing they would be there again for me the next night. I was done with the loneliness and the boredom and I wanted to spend my life with someone who shared my dreams and visions. I felt like I had done enough of the work of balancing the lower chakras, that I had a strong enough foundation to let someone in. My beautiful bestie, Alex, told me how she'd written a letter to the universe as a way of manifesting a wonderful man who she built a family with, so I figured I might give this a go. I knew the importance of writing things down, as it took the energy of desire out of my system, and into the world of form, but she told me I had to be very specific about what I wanted from this union, 'make sure you ask for it all darling, don't leave anything out." I figured I had rummaged around myself enough to be able to really ask for what I wanted, but the key was, did I feel like I deserved it?

I wrote my letter to the universe, sealed it with love and put it away in a little box along with crystals, images and words of everything I wanted to manifest in my life. I even slipped a picture of George Clooney in there for the hell of it – you can't blame a girl for trying! And then I forgot about it, and I got on with the job of healing my heart.

My letter read:

Dear Universe

I am so grateful for the beautiful children and wonderful friends that have blessed my life. I am ready to meet a wonderful man to share my life with. I want a man who is kind and beautiful in spirit. Someone who wants to be the best they can be in this world, and who shares the same values as me. I want him to be ambitious but also philanthropic, caring for the world and the people around him by actively showing support for environmental causes. He must be intelligent, with a good sense of humour, and handsome. I want a man who cares for himself in both a physical and an emotional way – someone who knows his own mind. He needs to be true and honest, but also open, generous and warm to those who are close to him. I want him to love me without question, with passion and desire. I want him to treat my children as if they were his own and be a fabulous influence in their lives, showing them kindness and compassion through his own actions.

And I want to love my new man with all my heart. I want him to be important to me, but not as important as I am to myself. I want to laugh lots, have fun, experience new adventures and make love often. I want our relationship to be easy, as if we were made for each other, so that when we meet, we will just know.

I trust in the divine universe in me to honour the love I can see.

With blessings, Dee xx

***

The fourth chakra is called Anahata and it is located at the heart centre, which is the seat of universal love. Individual consciousness is developed through the lower chakras when we define our being, and collective consciousness is developed through the higher chakras. These serve to expand the self. However, it is love that sits at the heart of the chakra system and helps to redeem us to infinity.

"How do you spell love?" asked Piglet
"You don't spell it, you feel it," – said Pooh

– A.A Milne

Love opens with feelings. When the heart is open, we feel everything in life, all the good, bad and ugly feelings, and we have to learn how to stay open while we experience the ups and downs that will inevitably come our way. When the heart chakra is balanced, and we accept life as it is, we are able to enjoy wonderful relationships and intimacy with a partner, without one or the other person shutting down or reacting in a way where they do not take responsibility for their emotions. When we have an open heart, we are willing to feel it all, and then let the story go. But for many people, myself included, when the heart has suffered so much trauma, they shut down the minute they face a difficult situation. They usually become fearful of receiving the love they so desperately desire, as a result of the rejection and suffering, that still unconsciously traumatises them. For me, the work of healing the heart chakra was very much rooted in self-love. As a woman who had a tendency to be co-dependent, I was very willing to give love to everyone else, but this only left me feeling depleted and empty inside, and disappointed in others when a relationship came to an end. I had to somehow learn how to be in a relationship, where I didn't over give, and where I was able to allow the other person to fully show themselves and not try to fix them. And that's challenging for me, as I'm very quick to see what others can't, so I go diving in when sometimes I need to stand back and create space and allow the other to step in, without trying to fix them. Most people in life, young and old, go through periods when the heart is wide open, and experience great joy in life, such as falling in love or having children. But we also go through periods when we close our hearts, like when someone dies, or a relationship ends badly, and we shut down, and feel very lost and rejected. This is all very normal human behaviour, but what defines us is how quickly we can move through the ups and downs of life, and come back to the centre, to peace and to harmony.

In Jungian psychotherapy[23], the process of individuation continues with the marriage of the internal female and male archetypal energy, which are known as the anima and animus. Just as the Shadow Self can be projected onto others in a relationship if it is not owned and integrated, so too can the characteristics of the anima and animus. So, if a woman does not own the masculine characteristic that she sees in the cultural stereotype of the perfect male – such as strength, power and chivalry, then she projects these romanticised states onto her male relationships, which gives the man very little room to hide from his obvious faults. Unless he's George Clooney, of course! And if a man doesn't own his own feminine side, he may well project an idealised female nature onto his partner, which could be an overly passive or sexualised version of the modern independent women. By balancing masculine and feminine energy, we can enter into relationships with the opposite sex with more realistic expectations and a freedom to show our true selves. This has become more essential in modern society, where women are taking on traditionally male roles in the workplace and divorce rates are skyrocketing. I believe this has to do with our persona and our social identity. Social identity is the ideal picture of ourselves that we present to the world. So, if we hold ourselves up as the brave, powerful male hero, or the good, obedient girl, we set about creating relationships based on this idealised image of who we are. But, as we discovered in the work of the shadow through the second

146

chakra, we are more than just the persona. The self is made up of the conscious and unconscious mind, and to become whole and evolve as a being we need to integrate the shadow and the persona, as well as other archetypes, into the self. The anima and animus hold the collective consciousness of what it means to be male and female, and it is highly influenced by our culture, our parents and by mythology. This is why women marry men who are just like their fathers.

The way we relate to our internalised feminine and masculine energy comes from how we were treated as children by our parents. It'll therefore be no surprise for you to learn that most of my male partners have had issues with addiction, just as my own father did, or that I inherited issues concerning denial and control from my mother. This imprint from our primary carers runs deep and influences how we communicate with the world. The archetypal female from mythology and religion also influences us. The universal mother has appeared in the myths and stories of our ancestors as the goddess, the semi mortal, the hero and the demon, to name just a few. Jung observed that it's these archetypes that appear to us in our dreams and fantasies. However, over time we have become more separated from the knowledge and wisdom of the divine mother, especially in the West. We operate in a modern system that is highly individualised and is orientated around material value. The inner value of human love has been forgotten in the mainstream, and we have lost touch with the nurturing embrace of the divine feminine. Instead, we have lived under the rule of dominant masculine energy, which is characteristically powerful and strong, but also divisive. And our beautiful planet is hurting because of it. Only those who dare to open their hearts and embrace a new way of being will ride out the storm, as the divine feminine rises to take a more active role in all our lives, and on the world stage.

There are many ways in which we can become more in touch with the divine feminine within, and one of the easiest ones is to listen to your heart. Let your heart be the guide that shines the light on everything you do. Listen to it, feel it. Honour thy heart and it will honour you back. When something feels right, your heart will show you its truth. We have to stop allowing the mind to run the show, and start training it, so that it works in union with our feeling hearts.

***

"Your heart is the softest place on earth. Take care of it."

– Nayyirah Waheed

It's not possible to have love without loss. This fact is one of the greatest struggles of the heart. And the balance between the need to attach and be free is a very delicate one. We must accept that to experience great love, we will also discover great sorrow and grief. The two walk together hand in hand. And the expansion of the heart comes from both sides of the dance. It doesn't mean that all relationships will end in doom and gloom, what it means is we need to have a healthy appreciation that the heart's desire to attach in relationships is just as strong as the soul's desire to be free. This was powerful learning for me. In my relationships, I have always been very consumed by my man of the moment. The type of men I used to date always seemed to want my constant attention, as much as I expected theirs. But now I had a new framework of understanding that gave me an opportunity to really think about what I wanted from a romantic union. I had dined out on the notion of romantic love for years. The idea of boy meets girl and falls in love and lives happily ever after. But the work of the heart chakra had prepared me for another way.

"The heart chakra is about bonding. Unintegrated parts of ourselves that are not bonded into the heart with love will seek bonding elsewhere."[24]

The truth is we bring into our world the parts of ourselves that we are not willing to see. So, the anger that I failed to own for so long came back at me through my daughter's fiery temper. And so did my depression. I was unaware that my soul was deeply depressed; my denial of the depths of my grief and my insistence that I had ridden the wave and was OK clung to me. But I couldn't avoid what my outer world was showing me. I was surrounded by people who were, for many different reasons, suffering from depression. They seemed to come to me for comfort, and I couldn't ignore the fact that mental health problems were something that ran deep in our family wound. My father had bouts of depression spurned on, no doubt, by excessive drinking. Although alcohol gives people an initial buzz, depression is one of the key side effects when it starts to leave the body. This is why I suffer so badly if I drink too much because it brings darkness with it and forces me to face the demon of depression.

By mid-August 2015, I was feeling pretty down in the dumps with my life again, even though I had an amazing summer travelling to Thailand and Ireland, doing the things I loved. I thought I was making progress, but healing is like a dance where you take two steps forward five steps back, and I still couldn't shift this fog in my heart, that lingered from my visit to my ancestral roots. Thus, I went to see one of my witchy-poo friends, Jenny, for a soul reading, as the cards always made me feel better, and gave me a little seed of hope to work from, especially when I was feeling a bit stuck and wasn't able to find my own way. As Jenny laid out the cards and tuned into my soul, I could see her mind ticking over doing a few mental somersaults as she spoke to her "people upstairs", "So, they're telling me that your main issue is control. You're not allowing life to flow; you're still holding on. Your mother is in denial, she is fearful of this world and doesn't want to see beyond what her eyes tell her." As Jenny did my reading, something clicked inside. I went very quiet as I allowed my awareness to decipher what she was telling me, and my inner voice whispered, "She's not talking about your actual birth mother, you know, she is talking about your internal mother. She's talking about an aspect of you." Jenny went on to say, "I sense so much inner pain Dee, so much pain." I could see her body actually contort as she shuddered as the feeling passed through her. She went on to say, "There is so much heartache from past love. You are exhausted from it all. It is draining you almost to the point where you could have ME."

Then she said, "Dee, you have to stop associating pain with love. Love does not feel like this."

That was the mic drop moment, as I looked up at her vast blue eyes and she could see that her message was hitting home. My eyes started to well up as I said, in a barely audible whisper, "You know my given name is Dolores, it means sorrow or pain. It comes from one of the titles given to Mother Mary." As Jenny nodded her head and acknowledged my vulnerability, my heart started to open and I began to share some more. "Since I have been able to speak, I have never let anyone call me by my full name: Dolores. Hearing the name used to send chills down my spine. I think it's because it reminded me of all the pain and suffering that I carried into this world." As we sat in silence for a few more minutes and I allowed the enormity of what was being revealed to penetrate every cell in my body, I looked up into Jenny's piercing blues eyes again, which seemed to have a way of drawing you in. Like a little child seeking validation to a question, already knowing the answer, I asked, "Do I need to go and heal that pain?" And she nodded at me and said in a very matter of fact way, "Yes, Dee, you do."

I sat outside in my car for another 30 minutes unable to hold back the tears. I felt very small, scared and alone; I kept replaying her words in my mind, "Dee you have to stop associating pain with love. Love does not feel like this." Then the little girl inside of me asked, "What does real love feel like then?" And I cried some more as I realised, I didn't have the answer.

Over the next few days, I started to process what Jenny had told me, and review my life with this newfound wisdom. I saw how the choices I made in life were driven by this false sense of love. It was all starting to make sense, the reason I had had so many crap relationships and experienced so much sorrow in the name of love, was because my love radar was completely off-kilter. And the only way I was ever going to understand what love truly feels like, is if I learnt to love myself fully. And that meant going deep into the pain of the past, that I had carried into this life.

"Since the need for love is so strong in the excessive heart chakra, there may be poor boundaries and poor discrimination. We may fail to discern when a relationship becomes abusive and live in the fantasy bond where everything is just fine."[25]

I went into the pain by focusing on yoga postures that opened my heart and released some of the painful memories that were locked inside me. Every part of my body hurt when I did these back bending postures: my arms felt weak, my shoulders felt stiff and I thought my spine might break in two. I often left my mat sobbing and there were times when I thought I would stop breathing altogether. But I got on my mat each day determined to face whatever lay in the stillness of the pose.

If you do not have a regular yoga practice, but want to work on opening your heart, a safe way to do this is to lie down on your back supported by a cushion under your spine. You can then bend your knees or keep them straight – whatever is more comfortable. Open your arms so that they rest on the ground at shoulder height, and your body is in a T shape. Now just be. Stay in this position for up to 10 minutes, or longer if you are comfortable, and resist the temptation to move unless you feel real discomfort (then, of course, you must readjust yourself). As you allow the body to settle, observe the sensations of the breath as you relax into this submissive position in order to receive. Try not to fight any feelings or sensations that come your way. Be gentle and kind to yourself. When it's time to come out, roll gently onto your right-hand side and stay there for a few more moments as you blink your eyes open and bring awareness back to the whole self.

As I started to release some of the memories from the past, through my yoga back bending process, I created the space to dream again, and I used shamanic journeying and sound healing, to get a sense of what my heart was calling. A shamanic journey takes you into a dream-like state, where you open up to the wonders of the unconscious mind, and my journeys always took me through a jungle over a bridge deep into the wilderness. Little did I know that I would find myself standing on that bridge for real a year later and that all the yoga and energy work was preparing me for big changes to come. As I started to listen to my heart's desires, I became increasingly aware that I no longer wanted to live my middle-class suburban dream in St Albans. It just felt like that didn't fit me anymore, but I had no idea what the alternative was. As I pondered on my future, Fionn and I enjoyed the last few days of the school summer holidays in beautiful Swanage, a small seaside fishing village nestled in the Isle of Purbeck in Dorset – a place that has a magical, romantic, unspoilt energy to it. It is home to lots of artists and creative folk, and we stayed with my dear friend, Connie, chilling out and soaking up the earthiness of our surroundings. We went for walks on the beach, swam in the sea and wandered in the countryside, doing our best to dodge the intermittent bursts of rain typical of British summertime.

"Sit in the ocean.
It is one of the best medicines on the planet."[26]

I was starting to find great appreciation in the simple things in life, such as days out with friends, playing by the river and having easy, uncomplicated fun. This was something that had been missing from my life for so long. I felt like I finally had the energy to give my beautiful son the love and attention he needed. Previously, I'd been battling with my grief so much that I'd struggled to do this. It was hard enough to get through the days, let alone muster up anything extra. But as I started to spring back to life, I realised that my heart was screaming out for fresh air and fun. I needed the outdoor life. I thought long and hard about what it was that made me so happy and passionate about life when I travelled. My passion was fed by visiting new places, meeting new people, experiencing new cultures and eating amazing foods, but it was also about being outside in nature. I loved being by the ocean or in the mountains or the desert – anywhere that isn't contained within four concrete walls. I had this strong desire to want to feel it all again. I longed to feel the wind in my hair, the rain down my back, the sand between my toes and the sun on my face. It was like I needed to feed my soul with the elements. I was done with being stuck inside the protective four walls of my house, now I wanted to be outside and living. I knew I needed to go elsewhere to find my peace, I just didn't know where to go.

"If you always do what you always did, you will always get what you always got."

– Albert Einstein

As the long lazy days of summer drew to a close, I also started to question what type of relationship I wanted in the future. I had put my intentions out in my letter to the universe, but I still wasn't sure what I wanted from a man. Challenging all my preconceived ideas about marriage and love certainly made for an interesting time. Up to that point in my life, I had only ever dated English or Irish guys who were always a few years older and normally tall, giants of men who fitted my template of being nice looking, funny and reasonably smart – I use that term loosely for some of them! But I suddenly realised how dull that was making me sound. It's like sticking your hand in the sweetie jar and only ever picking the orange cream when there's a whole host of exciting possibilities out there. It was time to reprogram my thinking. I knew I wanted to meet someone who was completely different. If I'm honest, my taste in men had been somewhat questionable! I often entered into relationships consciously thinking: *What on earth am I doing here with this guy?* But the strong need to attach often dominated my senses, and I know I stayed way longer than was healthy in some relationships so I could feed my desire to fix others. Thankfully, through working on myself, I know I'm no longer like that. Whoever comes into my life next will be there for all the right reasons. It was time to step into my truth and live a life worth living.

Chapter 12

Facing The Fear

❖

"It you do not change direction you may end up where you were heading." - Lao Tsu

There are 69 acronyms for fear on Google and my favourite one is: *Fuck Everything And Run!* I guess you could call me the type of person who is slightly averse to stepping out of their comfort zone, and this was starting to become very apparent as I began to face my fears. You see, I never saw myself as someone who wasn't brave. I grew up as the strong one in our family, so to be faced with so much fear felt weird. I couldn't quite put my finger on whether it was an age thing, a grief thing, a childhood thing, a need to want to control everything kind of thing or all of the above. But there was no denying that since Tony had died, whenever a *situation presented* itself, where I needed to make a change, I went into denial, or convinced myself everything was fine, or I pirouetted around the issue. One minute I might decide to go in a certain direction, and the next I might reverse that decision, it was like my mind was flip-flopping all the time, and when it did I always knew there was an element of fear at play. Fear is the great trickster that keeps us separated from our true nature, as the monkey mind convinces us of all the things we can't do. It keeps us trapped in a world of limitations, rather than allowing us to explore the world of infinite possibilities which in truth is how we are designed to live. But our monkey minds keep us stuck in the programmes and exhaustive stories that we invent for ourselves, and it is these stories that tell us we're not worthy enough, or smart enough, or brave enough or have enough resources, so we hold ourselves back from achieving all the things we want to achieve in this life.

I kept finding myself falling into this trap, as the fear took centre stage, and stopped me from moving forward. The reason I was stuck and couldn't move forward was that I was afraid of the unknown. I remember this feeling only too well from my school days. I was always the girl on the outside looking in. I was so frightened of rejection that I never put myself out there with the 'in crowd', although they would have happily welcomed me. I can now see how I held myself back from having fun. I sabotaged having fun because I didn't feel worthy of friendship, and it's very sad to feel this way as a child because it's time that you can never get back. Indeed, when it came to picking the subjects for my A Levels, I distinctly remember choosing the ones my teachers wanted me to do, over the ones that I actually wanted to do. I wanted to write and study English literature. My heart wanted to devour the books of Shakespeare and write beautiful stories. I remember my English teacher at the time reading a verse from Romeo and Juliet and asking the class if anyone knew the significance of the piece. He said if we understood the depth of this piece, we should really study English. Nobody put their hand up, but I knew the answer. I knew the verse he read was a soliloquy, which is a speech where the character speaks to themselves, that highlights their inner thoughts and feelings. I use soliloquy all the time to write my books, and even at that time, my inner voice was saying, "Dee, you love English, you want to study literature and become a great writer. Put your hand up."

Writing was all I ever wanted to do. But my monkey mind said, "*Who do you think you are? You're not gifted at writing, your vocabulary is not vast, you don't speak nicely, how could you possibly be a writer?*"

At the time I was too afraid to shine, so I sat with it and shrivelled in my seat when he revealed the answer. My heart felt pangs of disappointment because I had betrayed myself and didn't step into my light when I could so easily have shown myself. I went on to study statistics, economics, and geography, which led me down a career path in media and business. It wasn't what my heart wanted but I had a great career in a creative industry, though I always felt mildly jealous of the copywriters and journalists when I thought about how different my career could have been if I had only followed my heart.

My life after that was littered with many moments when I was too afraid to show myself. I remember walking away from many business meetings wishing I'd had the courage to say what I really wanted to say. And the nagging voice of recrimination usually came to me at the end of the day when I was in bed, as I chewed over the events of the day and the silent voice in my head would say, "*Dee, why didn't you say x, y or z?*" It happened a lot when I worked at the BBC. There were lots of 'big' voices there and endless hours of debate. I used to say that an attempt to make a decision at the BBC was akin to the start of a good conversation. Everybody had an opinion and they all wanted to have their say.

"*Understand me.*
I'm not like an ordinary world.
I have my madness,
I live in another dimension
and I do not have time for things
that have no soul."

– Charles Bukowski

By late September 2015, I had a date with destiny when I got to face my fears and flip myself upside down, quite literally, when I attended a yoga workshop at a top London studio with my friend, Alex. The workshop was called, "Facing the Fear On and Off the Mat" and I was in a room full of 100 bendy yogis all dressed in the same Lulu Lemon pants and a bit too keen to outdo each other for my liking. I promised my friend I'd go along with her, but secretly I was shit-scared because I really didn't like back bending workshops – they made me feel very vulnerable, and I knew it was going to be hard for me, to be honest, I was a bit of a wimp when it came to pushing my body to the extreme. Part of me kept thinking, "OMG what if I have a tantrum and storm off. Or what if I shout at the teacher and tell her to fuck off if she tries to push me too hard"; I'd been known to do this before. Or what if I burst into tears if it all got too much, which would be totally uncool and not good for my ego. All my childhood insecurities started to surface, and they were all pointing to not being good enough. I was still in victim mode, still believing I was not worthy to be there, and I knew something needed to change. All my inner yucky stuff came out on the yoga mat, to be seen, including my competitive streak, which wasn't always pretty. It turned me into a little bit of a basic bitch, as I compared myself to the younger yogis, who seemed to effortlessly stick their legs over their heads. You see I wanted to be the best in class, but I wasn't a natural yogi, my body just wasn't built like a piece of string, and no matter how many times I tried to force myself into these extreme positions, my hips would creak, my shoulders would crack, and my spine would spasm, so I decided my body clearly wasn't designed for this kind of stuff. I'm actually super muscular and not naturally bendy, so when I first started yoga practice, I could barely hold my arms out to the side for any length of time without them shaking like crazy and aching all over. It took me years to get any sort of fluidity in my body, and I guess I was a bit envious of people who just walked into a studio, flopping into poses naturally, because it sure as shit didn't come naturally to me. So, I was sulking inside before we even started the workshop, and secretly looking for the exit, but then Alex made sure we got there early so we could be right up front, and I wouldn't be able to escape everyone else's gaze and my own scrutiny. I had a word with my inner critic to be nice, because she can be a bit harsh at times, and as the teacher glided in, my stomach did a number on me and I knew I was in trouble. She was a bit of a celebrity teacher and spent the whole workshop telling us, "Yes you can, yes you can, yes you can", when my entire body wanted to scream back, "No, I bloody can't". And there lieth the problem. I had this inner defiance that needed breaking down. It was my inner critic that refused to budge so that I could open up to the possibilities of my heart. My fear presented as extreme stubbornness, and it kept me in an analytical space where I looked for every excuse I could find to get out of something. I kid you not, there is a part of me that is stubborn to the core, almost immovable, and will go to any lengths to prove she's right. I've even been to a doctor to have him examine my body so I could make excuses for why I couldn't do some poses. In my defence, the doctor confirmed I have remarkably long thigh bones for a woman of my height which could explain why I can't do some moves, so I have that excuse verified and pull it out every now and again when I refuse to say, "I can"!

During the workshop, the teacher described the moment of moving out of fear as the moment of integration. It's the moment of awareness where we say, "I can" and also *feel* we can. It's the moment in a handstand when the fear of falling stops you from getting to the top, but you say, "I'm going to get to the top and do it anyway, and so what if I fall, I can always get up and try again." It's the moment the body releases any effort and softens into the pose. If you practise yoga, you will understand this feeling, it's when the body relaxes and stops holding on and you almost feel like you are the pose. You are not doing the pose, rather the pose is inside of you and it feels effortless. The point of integration is where the mind and heart come together as one. It's that split second when the mind stops controlling – there's that word again – and the union takes place to achieve the heart's desires. It is where all the groundwork and will of the lower chakras meets the effortless energy of the higher ones.

Throughout the workshop, we did lots of little poses to build up to the big move, which was to drop back into a very deep backbend, which quite frankly was a bit beyond me. My friend, Alex, was having none of it and kept saying, "Just do it, Dee, you can do it." And after a few false attempts, spurred on by her loving encouragement, I said, "Fuck it" and completely let go. I flew back and I did it. I fell back from Ustrasana (camel) to Urdhva Dhanurasana (full wheel) and marvelled at my body's capability to go beyond the limits of my mind. I felt so empowered because I knew at that moment, I'd stepped off my, "I can't do" attitude and into my, "I can do" way of being, which is where I wanted to be. It's these little things in life that break us out of our limitations and allow us to believe in new possibilities. Our fears are hidden so deeply behind the stories we tell ourselves, and the story is always a way of disguising the fear. The thing with fear is, when we face small challenges and rise above them, we build confidence and belief in life. It's as if we boost our internal bank of courage, making us more prepared for when we have to deal with the really difficult things in life. But if we never go to this place...if we only ever stay in our comfort zone and play things safe, we lack the skills and bravery to face the big stuff when it comes our way, such as sudden death, illness, redundancy or divorce. So, my advice is, don't live life in the slipstream, every now and again go out and do something that scares the shit out of you, and try to have fun doing it.

Another thing that fear teaches us, is that it is OK to not always have the answer. It teaches us to get comfortable with the unknown. The greatest inventions and achievements in life never end up as they were originally intended. That's why they're great because they kept evolving and changing to become better. They didn't stay stuck. When we get comfortable with the unknown, the outcome is usually far greater than what our small, limited minds could ever have expected.

Fear also teaches us about the stories we weave around our lives and the excuses we make because we're too scared to make changes. The workshop helped me see that I had been hiding out in my widow story for way too long. I had become stuck and was still playing the victim. I really needed to face what it was that I wanted: how did I want to live? I clearly wanted to move on, but I didn't know how. The truth was I was afraid of the unknown, afraid of what was out there if I just picked myself up and started to live again. It was time for me to stop trying to control life and to move to a place of absolute trust, where I could let go of attachment and learn to live in the flow.

AUTUMN 2015

By autumn I had reached the point of no return. I was in transition and was being prepared for a new life. I had made peace with my childhood and, through the work of the lower chakras, was beginning to think about my future and what I wanted from life. I had sent my letter out to the universe and was opening my heart to the divine feminine energy within. Through balancing the heart chakra, I had also opened up to the possibility of love. Now it was time to step into the higher chakras and into the divine wisdom of universal consciousness. I viewed harvest time as a chance to take stock and show gratitude for the blessing that had helped me to get to this point in my life.

It was time to prepare for my new life and do the work to leave the old one behind. It was time to open my ears and eyes to a new way of being through the work of balancing the fifth and sixth chakras. It was an opportunity to hear the internal voice within, to open up to the power of the third eye and my natural intuition, and to recognise the archetypal energy that was guiding my life and showing me what I needed to do to realise my dreams. In late October 2015, I spent a blissful week on a juicing retreat in Turkey and enjoyed the pleasure of solitude for the first time in my adult life since the children were born. I took time out of my daily life to reflect, rest and just be. It was heaven and I was able to see all the wonders of my life and appreciate the lessons I had learnt from my two magical children. I thought about my warrior child, Millie, whose passion and determination to fight for a better world are fierce and honourable. I also thought about my Zenlike son, Fionn, whose wisdom and compassion have always astounded me. My children helped me heal by reflecting back to me my own strengths and weaknesses. It was my love for them and my ability to finally see their anger, frustration and wisdom *as an extension of my own* that helped me heal the wounds that lingered in my soul. Healing the mother/child bond was about stepping into a place where I no longer felt attached to my suffering. It was the lesson I needed to learn from the third noble truth, which is, "Suffering ceases when attachment to desire ceases." That day came when my daughter within released me from the chains of disapproval and criticism and said, "Go out into the world and be the strongest, most courageous, most beautiful woman that I know you are." I will remember that day forever because it was the day I truly felt free.

And so, the Autumn of 2015 provided the gateway to a new me. At times I struggled and clung to the past, and at times I could see clearly and forged forward fearlessly with my plans. Along the way I was graced with these valuable lessons:

Our children are our greatest teachers. Listen to your children. They share so much wisdom in their childlike tantrums and in their innocence to see the truth.

When we detach from desires we will no longer suffer. Don't be discouraged if things don't seem to go your way. Just keep on moving forward and don't stop. When you know what you want the universe will give it to you at the right time. Let go of control.

In order to understand our patterns and behaviours, we need to recognise the sacred archetypal energies. As we open the third eye, we start to recognise the patterns and beliefs that form our unconscious subroutines, and we have a means of comprehending them by understanding the influence of archetypal energy.

We need to know that love heals all wounds. My purpose in life is to love and to be loved. I believe we are all bound by the one ultimate task and that is to be loved. When we heal our wounds and be ourselves, we open up to the divine grace of love and become a bright beacon that shines this light on the world around us.

Chapter 13

Finding My Voice

———————————— ❖ ————————————

"Man cannot be anything other than what he is. Whatever he is, he will create a society that mirrors him." – Jiddu Krishnamurti

The fifth chakra is called Vissudha in Sanskrit and this means purification. It is located in the throat region, which is the seat of divine communication. When we balance the throat chakra, we learn to speak and hear our own personal truth, which is our own unique connection to the divine. How we express ourselves changes as we evolve in life, so we need to slow down to listen to this quiet voice within. As we respect the calling to our true nature, we start to understand our life with a little more clarity, and compassion for all that we are and all that we have ever been. When we are not able to hear this inner calling, which is our heart's desire, our voice becomes louder to get our attention. We get stuck in loops and patterns of behaviour which only intensify over time until we get to the point where something drastic has to happen to bring us back into alignment with the heart's desire.

As I reflected on my own life lessons, I could see how my pattern of people-pleasing, meant that I was not able to speak up for what I truly wanted. And in truth, I had lived a life for others, and not for myself. And it was going to take a huge amount of courage for me to break a lifetime's worth of people-pleasing to finally manifest the life that I truly wanted. But by Autumn 2015, I finally had my breakthrough when I admitted to myself that I wanted to live abroad and travel. I was finally able to face myself and accept that I was not happy because I wasn't living the life that I truly desired. I realised I had been lying to myself my whole life because I always put others first, but now it was time to put myself first. And as I started to listen more intently to the voice within, she told me what I had to do to make my dreams a reality.

How we speak to ourselves and others is a clear indication of a healthy connection between mind, body and soul. When we are being true to ourselves, we are not afraid to let ourselves be heard. If we are not being true to ourselves, we silence ourselves and do not speak our truth, or we may have a tendency to dominate conversations or constantly interrupt others. The throat acts as a bridge between the heart and mind, so clear communication is key if we want to express ourselves fully in the world. Many women have experienced issues in this area, as we carry the wounds of the past, from times when our ancestors were not able to speak as freely as we can today. As we learn to free our voices again, we begin to unravel these stories from the past and heal these wounds that deeply affect our lives today.

One such story that ran through my blood, and still runs through many women today, is the story of persecution, and the fear of the sacred powers that a woman poses. There was something very primal within me that felt the bible stories that I grew up with were very misunderstood, by many, including myself for a very long time. It was only when I allowed myself to unravel and connect with my own divinity within that I could decipher what the scriptures meant to me. My understanding of the world and the mysteries is that they are always written in allegory, and that there are many layers and meanings that can, and will, be understood when we are ready to receive a certain message. The teachings of the divine union came to me through the story of creation when I was ready to interpret the metaphors that I believe are hidden behind the literal story of Adam and Eve. To me, the story of Adam and Eve is a story of duality, and how we all come to earth to learn about ourselves through the conflict of opposites. When we unite the opposing forces within ourselves, great transformation and change occur, and an alchemical process within allows for new creation to be born. We learn about ourselves through the similarities and differences that we see in the world, and that we see in others, and it is this 'difference' that opens us up to the blind spots that we have within. Most of us accept the aspects of ourselves that we like, and we navigate towards people who tend to have similar views. But we are less willing to accept the aspects of ourselves that we don't like, and so we are judgmental and not so kind to people who show us these traits. However, if we are willing to meet all of life with acceptance of what is, we can transform the experiences that we don't like into something we do like through the power of non-interference. When we understand the interconnectivity of all life and all experiences, we tend to be less reactive, to situations that we find challenging, and we learn to move through them with more ease and grace knowing that we are truly creating each moment through the union of heart and mind.

Over the years, my body had shown me that my fifth chakra was out of balance. I had regular bouts of laryngitis, which literally shut me down for weeks and forced me to listen to the quiet voice within. I also had an excessive fifth chakra, which meant I had a tendency to talk too much. It was my way of masking the emptiness inside. I often interrupted people in my eagerness to show love, and regularly drew the conversation back to myself when someone was talking to me. For example, if one of my girlfriends was telling me about a problem with their boyfriend, I couldn't just listen to them and be empathetic, I always felt compelled to turn the conversation back to me and show solidarity by talking about how I had experienced the same issue. It was as if their problems gave me a platform to air my own. I thought I was being empathetic and showing understanding and compassion by relating their story back to me, but what the universe was actually showing me was that I had a desperate need to listen to myself. This constant interruption and turning the spotlight back to myself was a mechanism I used for years. Finally, I was starting to understand it was an opportunity for me to open my eyes and ears to my inner self. The way I responded to others was not with empathy – it was with control. My control showed itself most poetically via my interactions with my warrior child, Millie.

In many ways, my children have been my greatest teachers, although I wasn't always so willing to listen to what they were saying, in the early days. After years of teenage turmoil, screaming matches over the breakfast table and endless retorts from Millie (that usually ended with, "You're not listening to me") I finally started to hear the message that life needed me to hear. Whenever I think of my children and the lessons they bring to me, I'm always reminded of this truly exquisite piece of writing from Kahlil Gibran in his book, *The Prophet*:

"Your children are not your children.
They are the sons and daughters of life's longing for itself.
They come through you but not from you,
And though they are with you yet they belong not to you.
You may give them your love but not your thoughts,
For they have their own thoughts.
You may house their bodies but not their souls,
For their souls dwell in the house of tomorrow, which you cannot visit,
not even in your dreams.
You may strive to be like them but seek not to make them like you.
For life goes not backwards nor tarries with yesterday.
You are the bows from which your children as living arrows are sent forth.
The archer sees the mark upon the path of the infinite, and he bends
you with his might that his arrows may go swift and far.
Let your bending in the archer's hand be for gladness;
For even as He loves the arrow that flies, so he loves also the bow that
is stable.

Millie had a fighting spirit just like me and it was very loud in her teenage years. As she battled with me to be heard, I battled to control life by filtering out what she was actually saying to me. For years I simply wasn't capable of hearing or responding to her feelings because I wanted everything to be OK. We were both absolutely exhausted by our own personal struggles with grief. Millie and I had travelled a long road together with our shared experience of death. She had to grow up fast and dig in deep when her dad died when she was only 11 years old. Her resilience astounded me, whereas I struggled a lot more, but we had a profound understanding of each other's pain. We had worked through all the grief with years of therapy, but there was this dark cloud over us and we were stuck in a pattern of not being able to communicate, which was hurting us both. The bond of love between us ran so deep that when anything challenged it, we both felt intensely wounded. Just when I thought I was making progress and working through my issues, I would end up projecting my anger at Millie, screaming at her the minute I came through the door after yoga, when I should have been all blissed out. I would have a complete temper tantrum about something totally unimportant, such as the dishes not being washed, or her room not being tidy. I found myself back in my old ways of conditioning and that nagging voice inside persisted with feeding me lies about the house needing to be perfect before I could be loved. Our interactions were at times explosive, and we were both shocked by the fierceness of what came out of our mouths. I didn't recognise the woman who was losing her mind and screaming at her daughter, I just knew that I wanted it to stop. Millie was and always will be my first great love in life, but I could feel the thread between mother and child pulling apart, and I didn't want her to go into adulthood hating me.

> "Every day we miss opportunities for making true connections because instead of listening and responding appropriately to our children, we respond only from our point of view and fail to make a connection to their experience."[27]

This pattern of fight vs control was also the pattern I had with Millie's Dad, Martyn, and my mother. I realised life was trying to show me that it was my pattern, not theirs. I had to take responsibility for all of my experiences and relate to my life from this new level of awareness. This happened in the most profound way when Millie asked if we could do family therapy, as the last few years had been particularly difficult between us and we were both feeling it. I wasn't convinced and believed it was Millie who needed therapy in order to address her behaviour towards me. This was on the premise that when she sorted out her anger and rage, we would be able to get along better. So, I firmly placed the responsibility onto her and denied what was really going on. I was not averse to having therapy, I just couldn't see it as my problem. And that denial was part of the issue.

It was my failure to look deeply at my issues that was the problem, this had nothing to do with Millie. Through her behaviour, she was teaching me about the rage, anger and sadness I was holding onto. The path to finally seeing this was truly profound.

In late October 2015, I travelled to Turkey to spend a week on my own at a juicing retreat. It was the first time I had spent an entire week on my own in my adult life since the children had been born, and it was blissful to take 7 days just for myself. I did absolutely nothing apart from resting by the pool and doing some gentle yoga, generally switching off from daily life. I needed to be on my own without the children, without anybody knowing my story, without anybody actually knowing me. This ability to just slip into my own mind and space for a while in peaceful anonymity was so long overdue. Most of the other ladies on the retreat were city high flyers who were stressed to the eyeballs and needed to detox from their boozy, privileged London lives. When we all met on the first evening to introduce ourselves, the overwhelming reaction from the group towards me was, "Why do you need to be here?" And it was a good question. I looked so chilled out and blissful that many of them wanted a piece of what I had. But the truth was, the health and peace I exuded were mainly on the surface, and I still needed to go deeper to heal the wounds of the past. I needed to go deeper to heal a lot of the anger and resentment I had towards Millie's father and I knew this anger was affecting my relationship with my daughter. I had done a mountain of yoga and spiritual practice to get to where I was, but I needed psychotherapy to go deeper. I categorically wouldn't be where I am today without the help of an amazing therapist Lynne, who took me by the scruff of the neck and hit me hard with the truth. It was Lynne who told me, *"Dee, you've done an amazing job to be where you are but you've had, what we call in the business, a spiritual bypass. You're not dealing head on with the deep-rooted issues of why you are feeling this way."*

Spiritual bypassing is the use of spiritual beliefs to avoid dealing with painful feelings, unresolved wounds and psychological issues. And it was becoming increasingly clear to me that I had misused spirituality as a way to avoid the painful messy truth that I was still very wounded by my past and had sidestepped a lot of my issues under the guise of new-age thinking. Spiritual bypassing is the shadow side of spirituality, and it presents as an overemphasis on the positives in life, it shows up as weak boundaries in relationships, through overly tolerant compassion, and delusions of having arrived at a higher level of being. Any spiritual path, Eastern or Western, that doesn't engage in a significant depth of psycho-emotional work leaves a person open to spiritual bypassing. And it's fair to say I was proficient at skimming the surface of all the new-age practices whilst never really going in deep. And the great irony is I connected to Lynne when I stepped inside a bloody Crystal shop. I mean, the universe must have been laughing out loud when that happened! I went looking for guidance, for something, that could help me rebuild my relationship with Millie, which by this stage was hanging by a thread. As I browsed the bookshelves, one of the girls at the counter asked if she could help, and I told her about my struggle with my daughter. She listened to me with love and compassion as I ranted on, and then she pulled out a number from her phone and said, "Give Lynne a call. She will help you". She obviously knew that I wasn't going to get what I needed from another shiny crystal.

In our first few therapy sessions, Lynne spoke to Millie and me together. She could sense the willingness to heal and the love we had for each other, but she could also see how my inability to hear Millie's feelings had left this vast vacuum between us. This inability to hear was actually my own inner child crying out to be heard. My inner world was showing itself in my beautiful daughter, and in my insistence on always being right. The projected rage I was experiencing in my interactions with Millie was an accumulation of my own inner anger that had generated over many years and been repressed from childhood. But it was also the yes/no attitude that was stifling the creative expression in me, and which was symptomatic of the fifth chakra being out of balance. It wasn't just my inability to see beyond black and white, right and wrong, yes and no, but I soon realised it was the basic reward system I used for my children and myself. I became increasingly aware that I was rewarding good behaviour and punishing bad behaviour, just as my mother and her mother had done, as well as generations of Irish mothers before that. And this was not how I wanted to raise my children or, just as importantly, these weren't the restrictions I wanted to give myself. If I wanted to live in a creative stream of consciousness, I needed to expand my thinking, which was stuck in a framework of a binary yes/no approach, and view life differently. I needed to train my monkey mind some more, I needed to stop insisting on being right all the time, and I needed to stop giving others the answers to life when I could barely work out my own shit.

Healing these deep wounds takes time, and while Millie carried on in therapy, it took me another 9 months of polishing my spiritual mirror, to come off my all-knowing pedestal, before I got to the core of my issues. And guess where the call for help came from? It came through the Crystal shop again, when I went in for a reading and the first thing they asked was, "Who's Martyn?" I explained he was Millie's dad who had passed away, and then they replied, "They're telling me you need to do some talking therapy around Martyn." Well, I nearly fell off my seat, and the moment I got home I called Lynne, and she laughed when I told her about my reading at the Crystal shop as she said. "Well Dee, I have been waiting for your call," and thank God she did, because I really needed her help to bring me back down from the heavens and into true reality.

As we talked over the coming months, Lynne helped me piece together my childhood story and helped me understand how connected life was, and how I was truly responsible for my interactions with Millie and the world I was creating around me. She brought me out of the clouds and into grounded reality, down from all the spiritual whoo-whoo that I was familiar with. She helped me make sense of what was really going on in my life and helped me break through all the love and light to see the crappy bits of life too. She made me face my co-dependency and my childhood trauma, and brought me down to earth, as I tried my best to avoid it all. She helped me see that true spirituality didn't live out in the stars but is found in the depths of our humanness, and how we relate to others. Lynne helped me reconnect to my heart and encouraged me to talk about my feelings, knowing that I would try to analyse everything which is the mind at play, and it was now time to get down and dirty with how things actually feel. Lynne truly understood the nature of human interaction and listened so intently to me, not just for me, but for herself too, and her example taught me how to *consciously listen*. To listen with open ears, to not interrupt conversations, and to allow time and space between words before I responded. I was all too aware of my eagerness to offer advice to others and in truth, I needed to sit with my own wisdom for a while and just go within.

I started to listen more intently to my children by pausing before I opened my mouth – which was hard for me to do, and it made a huge difference to our relationship. Rather than going into autopilot and jumping in to offer my opinion the minute they spoke to me, I gave myself time to breathe, asking myself, "Dee did you really hear what was said?" I found myself responding to my kids with so much more love and integrity than if I had just opened my mouth and let whatever was on the surface fly out. By pausing, I was able to communicate with them in a lot more depth. I noticed that my children carried the same tendencies as I do, so when I started to really listen to the words that came my way, I was able to observe myself in their language and see my own patterns play out in my communication with my kids. This helped me turn inwards and really look at the aspect of myself that was at play in the conversation, so I could work on that characteristic within me that I saw being reflected in others.

Chapter 14

Learning to See

———————————— ❖ ————————————

"We don't see things as they are, we see things as we are."
- Anais Nin

By the end of the year, I was beginning to see myself more deeply through the eyes of the world around me. By listening intently to my children's innate wisdom, I connected to my inner child, and by allowing my lifeforce to connect with nature, I started to unfold, and as I did, the world around me became more alive as I delved deeper into my heart. I was starting to access my inner vision and the wisdom that extends beyond my life here on earth, into the infinite possibilities of the universe within. And it was through this wisdom that my third eye opened to the wonders of the universe.

It is our vision that constantly creates the path for our future and liberates us from the past. This is the work of Ajna, the sixth chakra, whose purpose is to perceive and command our reality.

"As we enter the third eye we can see where we have been, where we are now, and predict where we are going."[28]

The third eye is the energy centre of our inner perception. It is the screen where we project our desires and learn about them through images, archetypes and fantasies. As we open the third eye, we begin to bring conscious awareness to these desires, and the light of reality to all that is within us. We start to recognise how the patterns that have occurred in our lives have been sent to teach us something fundamental about ourselves, and we have those 'aha' moments where everything seems to suddenly make sense. Jung's process of individuation continues into the sixth chakra when we start to integrate and recognise the archetypal energies that affect our behaviour. In her amazing work on the chakra system, Anodea Judith correlates each chakra to Jung's archetype.

1. The Root Chakra is the Earth Mother/Provider
2. The Sacral Chakra is the Lover
3. The Solar Plexus Chakra is the Hero
4. The Heart Chakra is the Healer
5. The Throat Chakra is the Artist
6. The Third Eye is the Seer
7. The Crown Chakra is the Sage/Master

When we enter the sixth chakra, we start to see the bigger picture. We start to see the world from many different perspectives as we integrate the energies of these seven inner guides to give us wisdom and wholeness. We learn to call upon their guidance in different situations and recognise their differing viewpoints. For example, the lover in you will see something very different to the artist in you. The artist may well approach a situation with a critical eye, whereas the lover may see it from a more accepting place. When we learn about the archetypes we learn about our true nature. We start to see where we identify heavily with one and less so with another, and we are able to examine how this has impacted our lives through the patterns that have occurred in the past. This awareness gives us the freedom to break these patterns and create new behaviour. Archetypal energy manifests in what Jung called complexes, or the things we do or think, even though we may know better. So, for me, this is that drink that takes me over the edge and makes me feel miserable the next day, or the critical voice that says, "You can't" when I know I can, or the doubt that filters in when I'm tired and feeling lonely. Also, we can embrace more than one archetype at any given time, which may cause conflict inside as different ones fight to be heard. When I'm battling with myself, I know it's often the archetypes at play. The artist in me may be crying out for solitude to write, whereas the lover wants to go out to play. Over the years, I have learnt the importance of honouring both, because if we punish and chastise the voice of an archetype, we send it into the shadow realm where it will manifest into our lives through behaviours that we project onto others.

When we spend time on the inner planes communing with ourselves, we find a strength of knowing that brings us into faith. Faith is the key that unlocks higher levels of consciousness but it can only be cultivated by you, it does not come from outside of you. I like to think of Faith as finding acceptance in the heart. And it asks you to meet yourself fully, with the knowledge that there is a force within that will hold you, if you allow it to. When the heart and mind work in unison with each other, the path within is illuminated, and you begin to create the life you want. The body becomes activated in such a way that you can feel it tingling, as the calling of the heart draws you in. But most of the time we are unable to claim this power for ourselves because we are so programmed by others that we believe things that are not ours, as we surrender to the mind control and mute the song of the heart. And when our hearts and minds work against each other we create resistance, which is stored inside the body, creating disease. Or we may react to this resistance and spew this energy out into the world. When we spew these forces into the world, they eventually find their way back. When this happens, you can do one of two things: you can learn about yourself as you meet yourself reflected in the story that triggered a response out of you, or you can charge it with more of the same and thus, create more. You learn about yourself by how you relate to these stories. However, if you can get beyond the story and just be with the energy when it rises on the internal planes, you can move through it much quicker and deal with the resistance in your own way.

"Come forth into the light of things, let nature be your teacher"

– William Wordsworth

We perceive life in a way which is unique to how we choose to process information. Most of the time this information comes as a stream of consciousness that we package up and access at a time when we are ready to receive the light codes within our body that enact on the information that we receive from the source. There are many ways to access this divine wisdom within ourselves, and when we work in harmony with nature and the world around us, the process of receiving a clear signal to the source of our being is easy. And when we connect to our own divine intelligence within, we begin the journey of faith in the most beautiful way through communing with our soul. There is such a purity to this connection because it is felt in the heart, it cannot be denied and it is strengthened whenever we connect to nature. The downloads from nature come while we are being wrapped in the essence of the elements, through the trees, the water, the rocks, the plants, the animal kingdom and through the air that we breathe. When we are connected to our hearts in this beautifully primal way, our bodies start to come back online and life becomes a very elemental, felt experience. When this happens, we cannot be contained by four walls or be spoon-fed information by others because our spirit just rebels. It was this rebellious nature of life that was calling me and asking me to consider another way of being, as I wrapped myself in love and asked my heart what it was that I wanted.

My heart longed for freedom, she longed for love and a life in nature. She longed to be outside the system, to be fully free to explore who I am and just be me, without the programmes and conditioning that came from my past. And it was in this space of deep love and appreciation for myself that I found I no longer wanted the Western dream that I had so longed for in the past. My daughter Millie was approaching 18 and her path was set: completing her A Levels and going off to university to study film and history. She had grown into a strong, independent woman. The past had sealed that fate for her and I knew she was primed for a bright future in England, living the life she wanted. But I wanted something different for Fionn and myself. It was now time to turn my attention to what was right for us. And something deep inside me knew that whatever it was, I was going to have to go on a long journey to find it. That something was my intuition.

"Intuition is the unconscious recognition of patterns. It is one of the four functions of Jungian typology – the others being sensation and feeling, related to the first two chakras, and thinking, which relates to chakra seven."[29]

Intuition is that little flicker in the belly, or that flutter of the heart, or that 'just knowing' – as I call it – when you feel beyond what is there with a level of certainty that is unexplainable. When we develop our intuition, we develop our psychic skills and our ability to see through the conscious surrender to the unconscious mind. This requires a huge amount of trust and practice as we learn to unscramble the messages that come to us. And, as with anything that requires practice, you don't always get it right! When we move into the higher realms of the sixth and seventh chakra we move beyond the realm of the individual self into a higher place of understanding and the collective consciousness.

13th November 2015 was a day that will forever remain in my consciousness as the day of two halves. It was the day the world witnessed Paris' pain as she was brought to her knees by violence and terror that made no sense. It was also the day I met Magic Marina, my mystical friend, who helped me piece together the story of my life, with a level of clarity that I had not known before. Like many Seers, Marina could read my energy field in the ethers. She brought into words the things that I knew in my heart, and her reading planted the seeds for the life that lay ahead of me. She could see me holding workshops in the future, and creating a safe place where others could learn. She spoke of how, as my body became cleaner from alcohol, food and negativity, I would become more intuitive and there would come a time when I wouldn't need to turn to others to illuminate the path ahead of me. She spoke of how I had a profound sense of duty and wanted to be the best I can be in this world, and this passion was bound by my understanding that everything is connected. And so, I began to visualise a new way of being for myself and my son, I knew I wanted to raise him in a more sensitive environment where children played outside in nature and didn't wither away indoors on their electronics frying their brains and killing their imagination. I wanted him to be schooled somewhere where they valued his individuality as much as they valued their league tables. I wanted him to live somewhere that protected his sensitive nature and said it was OK to be an individual. But most of all, I wanted him to be somewhere that had beautiful energy that could feed his soul. Also, I needed a time-out from it all. I needed to press reset, and deprogramme my mind before I could make a fresh start somewhere new with like-minded people. And I wanted to find love, a love that would last a lifetime, and there was something very primal inside telling me that I needed to journey deep within to find that love inside of myself before I could ever offer it to another. Thus, I set my intention on this new way of being, I visualised and prayed, and then I set it free. I gave my trust to the universe and waited.

"Sixth chakra development is usually referred to as spiritual awakening. We suddenly see with new eyes, experience profound insight, change our perspective and attitude, or receive a vision. It can happen any time in life, but like the light of most dawns, it is often preceded by darkness."[30]

And I was awakening. I was doing the work and awakening the woman inside who had been silenced for years. I was seeing with new eyes, hearing with new ears, and feeling again with a heart that was open. I had walked through the darkness of the soul, the darkness of grief and loss, of longing and anger and betrayal to find this new woman staring back at me in the mirror. It was now time for her to step back out into the world.

Chapter 15

Leaving The Past Behind

--- ❖ ---

"Darkness cannot drive out darkness; only light can do that.
Hate cannot drive out hate; only love can do that."
– Dr Martin Luther King, Jr.

On that same evening on 13th November 2015, I looked at my Facebook feed and cried as the world watched the horrors in Paris unfold as the heart was ripped out of the city of love in an atrocious attack on humanity that claimed the lives of 130 people and shone a spotlight on how divisive our world has become. And in that moment, I was called to action. I had stood by and watched so much suffering and conflict in the world, especially over the past five years. The depth of grief in my personal life was mine alone, but it was also a reflection of the depth of grief on our planet as our beautiful world cried out in pain from the destruction caused by us all. I was feeling the pain and suffering from Mother Earth through my own experience, and there was no denying this suffering. The evidence was so clear that even a blind man could see the truth. As a global community of 7.5 billion people, we seem to be hell-bent on killing our planet and killing ourselves. I felt a deep sense of duty after the atrocities in Paris, on the night of November 13th 2015, which profoundly affected me as I tried to make sense of it all, and explain it to my children who were scared of the world we were living in. Millie had been out at a nightclub in London at the time of the Paris bombings. When she arrived home at 4 am she fell into my arms like a small child. It seemed like the Paris attackers had achieved their goal because my beautiful, darling Millie was terrified. She had been dancing the night away at Café de Paris, a French nightclub in Central London, when the news of the attacks flashed up on the social media feeds that every young person seems to be addicted to these days. She watched, surrounded by the young French living in London, as they fell to their knees with grief, as they saw what was happening in their homeland. One moment they were dancing and having fun, the next they were on their knees crying. The pendulum of life had swung from joy to sorrow in that one split second. It is within these defining moments that transformation occurs. As Millie left the nightclub to make her way home, the city of London went into lockdown. The ripples of fear started to feed their way around the major capital cities of the world and they were put into a state of heightened security, in case further copycat acts were planned. The London Underground and bus services were pulled out of operation and Millie had to jump in a taxi to get herself back home to Hertfordshire. As I wrapped her in my arms to comfort her, I was reminded of the pain she felt when I told her the news of her father's death. It was as if that wound had been reopened and, as she drifted off to sleep, I knew I had to do something to ease the suffering.

It's difficult not to get consumed by the news at a time of tragedy when the horrors of terrorism monopolise every media outlet. I made a conscious decision to stop actively participating in the 'news' many years ago when I made a choice not to feed the fear and negativity that our news channels spew out on a daily basis. It doesn't mean I'm not compassionate and detached from world events because I am still aware. I am more aware than most, but my awareness comes from a place of love. I do not need to be fed the news with someone else's agenda all over it to feel what is going on in the world. I do my best to tackle these issues by living a conscious life, where I try to walk gently on the earth. This is how I am actively participating in the movement of global consciousness that is shining a light on the world in a time of darkness. And I believe we can all find another way of living when we free the mind from enslavement to the systems that we inherit from the past and allow ourselves to connect to our true nature. And from here, we get to create the lives we desire. The mind is such a powerful tool of creation and when the mind and heart work together, as one, we co-create with the earth, not taking from Gaia but nurturing and being nurtured by her. When it comes to people who do atrocious things in the world, if we do not give these people a platform to voice their hatred, then there is no platform to voice hatred. And your beautiful presence in this world IS the platform for you to be the change. If we empty ourselves of all hatred and lies, if we unlock the systems within and go deep into the state of our being, we cast out these voices within, so that they can never be heard again.

The next morning, Millie was glued to the social media feeds that were consumed with the events of the previous night in Paris. It was hard to avoid, and I struggled to understand any of it. I found it hard to comprehend how people could kill in the name of religion. To me, the bombings in Paris represented a historic moment, where people's minds were so horribly manipulated by a force that hides out in the shadows and pretends to be something that it is not. And this is both shocking and heart-breaking in equal measure because so many good people have faith in these systems that place control over them in the name of God. We have all innocently believed in the goodness of others without really seeing what is there, and when the veils come down and we discover the truth of what is, this shocks us to the core. When we finally discover the extent of this control, something awakens inside, which is a force of nature, that rises from the ashes and blazes with fury like no other because she has been lied to in plain sight. She is the divine feminine, the mother, the giver of life, and she will cut through every last drop of hatred and lies that is hiding inside of you. And she does it all for love.

This Love inside of you is beyond boundaries; it cannot be contained and it is constantly expanding and growing. No act of war, violence or injustice is ever done in the name of so-called religion, that pretends to be love. These terrorists are not acting out of love, they are acting out of fear. And fear is an energy, that can be changed.

"Everything is energy and that's all there is to it. Match the frequency of the reality you want and you cannot help but get that reality. It can be no other way. This is not philosophy. This is physics."

– Albert Einstein

In the ground-breaking book Power vs Force[31] by David Hawkins, the author shows how feelings vibrate energetically along a spectrum of consciousness, with the feelings of shame right at the bottom at 20KHZ and the feelings of enlightenment, which is ultimate consciousness, at the top at 700+ KHZ. When we force life, we are operating at lower energetic levels of consciousness, and living in a world of shame, guilt, apathy, fear, desire, anger and pride. But as we know from the basic laws of physics, force always creates a counterforce. When we step into the full power of life, we operate from higher energetic levels of consciousness and live in a world of courage, neutrality, willingness, acceptance, reason, love, joy, peace and enlightenment. Force can only exist if it is pushing against something – it cannot exist as a wholeness on its own, which is why the opposite of force, i.e. power, *will always win the day*. So, when we respond to tragic events in the news with fear, we may think we are being compassionate, but we are actually colluding with it because fear is low energy force. The only way to transcend fear is to act from higher levels of consciousness. I knew all about this through my own life, as I had sat in the depths of grief for so long. I have been there at rock bottom, at the lowest end of the energy spectrum, and I have pulled myself up and out of the other side. And the other side is where I walk hand in hand with my power of consciousness. I did this primarily through connecting to nature and through all the activities that I have described so far in this book. I lifted myself up from grief through the wounds of life that were controlled by fear and moved into the power of love, where I now live as a high energy being. And as I walk in the power of love, I am healing others just by being me. Because those of us who walk in the light change the vibrations of those who don't. And that is not some new-age hippie shit – that is the law of nature, which is ever-present on earth. We can change our reality, and our life, by being the change from one moment to the next, by being consciously aware of the decisions we make in our lives.

> *"Imagine all the people living life in peace, you may say I'm a dreamer but I'm not the only one, I hope someday you'll join us, and the world with be as one."*

– John Lennon

As 2015 drew to a close, I started to get a deeper sense of inner peace within myself. The rewards of my spiritual practice were beginning to show on the outside, as my body felt lighter and more expansive and a youthful glow replaced the grey sheen of grief that I had worn for so many years. There was no going back and I finally felt like I had the strength to leave the past behind. I found the courage to walk away from my old patterns of behaviour and learnt to balance the needs of the archetypal energies that presented themselves through me. I started to feel real compassion towards my daughter and saw my relationship with her as an opportunity to heal the mother/child bond in me. I found the angel within me through the zen-like spirit of my son, who revealed more understanding of life than any book, teacher or person that I have ever known. Both of my kids gave me hope that the evolution of mankind was moving forward, or should I say coming back to the truth which is unified in the wholeness of our being. And I stood shoulder to shoulder with my new tribe in the sisterhood of consciousness that was rising up and lighting the way for the world to be a better place. And this light was guiding me back home, back to mother India, back to my heart and the final journey on my path to healing.

WINTER 2015

It was in the beautiful icy stillness of winter that I came to the end of my search for a home. I'd found India again and my heart opened to the flow and showed me a new way of being. I spent a magical Christmas in the white sands of Agonda, South Goa, with my soul sisters, Jennifer and Alex, and experienced the freedom of living in the flow and letting go of control. India taught me how to be, and brought me into the seventh and final chakra on my journey of transformation. India taught me about non-attachment and opened me up to the universal identity of oneness. And India started to show me what true love really was.

As I entered 2016, I stepped into a new space of consciousness, which taught me how to live from the heart. I became more aware of myself through listening to my feelings and allowing my heart to guide me. When we live from the heart, the choices we make seem to be divinely orchestrated. And my heart told me that I needed to live in India. And so, with a renewed sense of purpose, I set about making the plans to move to India with Fionn. At times it was scary and I questioned what on earth I was doing, and at times when I sat in the quiet and contemplated everything that had happened to me in the previous year, it just seemed to make perfect sense. I knew I needed to let Tony go once and for all, and I knew that was intrinsically tied up in me finding myself and finishing my book. And, for some reason, I knew the magic would happen in India and the words would fly to me as they'd never flown before. I could just sense it. But in the face of the greatest change comes the greatest resistance and I faced lots of it from my family, especially Millie, who thought I had finally lost the plot. But with my strengthened will through the work of the lower chakras, I had the fight in me to face this demon of attachment. And from this new height of being, I could also see that this resistance wasn't theirs, it was mine. It was my ego at play. It was the frightened child that struggled to release the past. The battles I had with others were a reflection of my own inner battle to let Tony go. But I sat with it all with a renewed sense of knowing that I was doing the right thing.

Winter is a time for inner reflection, where the world stills itself, animals hibernate and the soul faces the cold and hard realities of life. We walk through a period of darkness as the days shorten, and we sit with the things that make us feel uncomfortable. But it is also the time when we finally break free from the cycles that hold us back. Doing this work is not easy, but doing it ultimately leads us to liberation. By the end of the winter, I took my first step on this path, and it showed me the following key pieces of wisdom:

To be in the flow you need to let go of control. And I knew this. I knew this deep in my heart. The times I allowed divine universal wisdom to guide me and let go of outlining, second-guessing and pushing against life, were the times when the magic happened. This happened without fail every single time.

The path of wisdom, meditation and morality was the way. This is essentially about looking, seeing and being in the world from a place of love. It involves everything we do, from how we eat, to how we speak, to how we make money. We feed these through our meditation practice as we gain wisdom to be the best we can be in this world. And there is no end. We keep on moving, growing and expanding.

To stay faithful to the heart, even in difficult times. The heart never fails you. Even when you are on your knees in the depths of despair, your heart will find a way to heal you. Your beautiful heart is your gift from God.

We need to walk through the darkness to see the light. When we are in tune with the world as it is, we cycle through the seasons with an appreciation that there will sometimes be darker times and struggles in our life. But once we learn to accept all aspects of our life we let go of expectations and become less attached to the outcome. We allow life to reveal itself organically, and by doing so we can transcend suffering and return home to our true nature.

Chapter 16

I'm Coming Home

❖

*"She had the soul of a gipsy, the heart of a hippie and
the spirit of an angel."*

On December 18th, 2015, my feet touched Indian Soil again for the first time in 25 years. I felt nervous about returning to the country that I had lost my heart to in my early twenties when I went backpacking around the world. I was scared that the young carefree girl I used to be had somehow become lost within me, and that perhaps the expectation of India did not match the sparkly memories I held in my heart. I kept thinking to myself, what if I stepped off that aeroplane and the magic had gone? What if I no longer had that sense of adventure and freedom that I had in my twenties? Returning to India felt like a test for my fragile soul, and I was scared that the adventurous beautiful girl I used to be was gone forever, lost in the abyss, and I wasn't sure my heart could cope with such disappointment. But the moment I stepped onto Indian soil, I felt an awakening inside, it was like the lights had switched back on and I felt alive again for the first time in aeons. I suddenly felt this deep longing inside of me that had been missing for aeons. As I got off the plane, Mother India wrapped her loving arms around me, as she called her child home.

As I stood in the long queue at immigration laughing at the endless paperwork, and mind-bogglingly crazy and inefficient Indian system, I found myself softening for the first time in years. The 90-minute drive down to the fabulous hotel on Agonda Beach in South Goa felt like a trip down memory lane, as all the love for this beautiful country came flooding back, and I remembered all the good times that this country had given me as the memories of that time replayed in my heart, mind and soul.

We arrived at our boutique resort at sunset, to a golden haze all around as the sun kissed the Arabian Ocean; this was my kind of paradise. The beautiful beach huts were built on the sand with a veranda overlooking the ocean, a dressing area suitable for my teenage fashionista and a stunning outdoor bathroom. The restaurant spilt out onto the beach, where you could sit on a daybed while watching the sun go down, and even though it was Christmas and peak season for tourists, the beach was pleasantly quiet. The vibe was calm and laid back, just how I liked it.

We soon got into our groove and settled into the chilled Agondan vibe. We spent our days lazing on the beach and mooching along the main street to buy knickknacks from the local traders, haggling over 10 rupees and getting into the Indian way of bartering for everything. By night, we enjoyed the delicious Goan cuisine in one of the beach shacks as we watched the sun go down and the sky dance in shades of pink and orange, marvelling at the spectacular show from Mother Nature. This was my kind of Christmas. I was on an amazing beach with my beautiful children, my two beautiful friends and their families, and I didn't have a care in the world. I could taste the freedom. I felt like my search was over. I can't quite explain it, but I just felt happy to be. I felt aligned to my inner self, as my heart opened and the magical sands of Agonda beach carried me back to my true self. And that self shone through me in Goa. My friend Jennifer commented on it, "Dee," she said, "I've never seen you come so alive. You look so light and beautiful."

It was true. I was alive in Goa. It was my special place. By the end of the holiday, everyone was teasing me and calling me the Christmas fairy because I used to light up the place with my megawatts smile, just like the locals. Our collective mantra for the holiday was, "I'll go with the flow". We didn't plan or organise anything in particular, we just went with what came at that moment and found ourselves wherever we were meant to be. We were at peace in the moment and ready to receive our blessings. Following years of struggle, I was beginning to see the simplicity of life when you stop controlling everything and start to allow life to just be. I really felt India was trying to teach me another way to live. She was teaching me to trust and to be open to the world of possibilities beyond the limitations of my mind. She was teaching me a lesson in not having to try so hard. The girls could see the transformation in me. As they went off to yoga and tried to coax me along, I said I really didn't feel like I needed it. I was happy to stroll up and down the beach and be on my own. I didn't want any outer influences to feed me, I wanted to be guided by the healing properties of the sand and the sea. It was quite remarkable considering I was an avid Yogi and practised five times a week, but once I opened my heart and listened to it, I couldn't deny what she wanted. I did, however, show up to one class. This was mainly because I'd promised Jennifer I would go with her one morning, and I always keep my promises. The teacher handed around a bowl with small pieces of folded paper that contained inspired words inside. We were invited to select a word and set our intention for our practice that day on whatever the word was. The words themselves were random, and I had no idea what I was picking up. Imagine my surprise when I unravelled my piece of paper to find the word 'control' written on it. I realised it wasn't random at all – it was divinely orchestrated. Of all the gazillions of words in the universe, I picked the one that was holding me down and keeping me blocked. Control. It was perfect. The universe was showing me I was meant to be in that yoga class on that morning in December in magical Goa. I was exactly where I was supposed to be. And this is how India taught me. She kept showing up to remind me that life only ever happens in the moment when we let go of control and start living in the now. I knew it. The card knew it. Life knew it. And my blessing for going with the flow was meeting David.

David showed up one afternoon right out of the blue, quite literally, in a holistic centre called The Space, which was situated outside Agonda beach on the Palolem to Agonda Road in the most idyllic spot overlooking the jungle. I took a trip out there one afternoon with Jennifer, Alex, and the two boys – my son, Fionn, and Alex's youngest son, Spike – to grab some food in the vegetarian café situated in an enchanted garden overlooking a field full of water buffalo. The Space was a haven for healers and therapists, who came from all over the world to hang out and run workshops and retreats. The maze of rooms, set in a beautiful old Portuguese mansion, was full of interesting trinkets and health foods to buy, and there was a large Yoga Shala in the jungle garden out the back. It was the perfect place to rejuvenate, meet like-minded people and eat great cakes! As the children played by the fountain in the garden on the front veranda, Jennifer and I wandered around the shop and read about the various therapies on the notice boards dotted around the place. I picked up a leaflet on myofascial release massage and as we poked around the various rooms in the back of the house, I noticed a rather handsome guy coming out of a room. We struck up a conversation with him and I asked if he knew about myofascial massage.

"Yes, I'm the therapist," he replied. "I'm David."

He talked about the benefits of the myofascial release technique and I was drawn in by his enthusiasm and gentleness. I had a niggling feeling there was something important about him. Later that evening, I spoke to Jennifer about it. Jennifer was like my spiritual sage, and I turned to her whenever I needed to discuss anything to do with my spiritual growth or affairs of the heart. I trusted her wisdom implicitly, it felt divinely aligned, like she was speaking directly to my soul. She was able to read me well, she could see all my insecurities that were often hidden, and our friendship has grown over the years as we've tried to help each other, as we both went through our own personal ups and downs. When I told Jennifer that I thought there was something special about David, she smiled and said knowingly, "He couldn't take his eyes off you. There's definitely a connection there!"

I laughed at her and replied, "Don't be so stupid, he's gay. The good-looking ones always are."

"I'm telling you, he's not, and he liked you, Dee."

I think my lovely Jennifer was trying a spot of matchmaking! She knew my pain and loneliness and wanted me to find love as much as I did. As I laughed off her comments there was that little niggle of intuition inside that just wouldn't go away. There was something important about David. Then I remembered my reading with Magic Marina and her parting words to me, "Who's David?"

I was here in South Goa about to find out. I didn't tell the girls about Marina's vision, that would have sent them into overdrive, but I did book in for a massage a few days later so I could check David out a little more. The treatment was absolutely amazing, and David was pretty damn amazing too. He had a serenity and gentleness that belonged to someone who truly loved what they were doing, and I felt the healing powers from his touch. So, when I came back from my treatment all glowing and full of smiles, Jennifer was waiting and uttered a rather knowing, "Well?"

I just laughed at her again, but I could tell she had plans for me! David and I became friends. He was quite unlike any man I had ever met. He has strong feminine energy and is sensitive and compassionate to others. Not the usual red-blooded alpha type I seemed to attract. He cares deeply for the world around him and conducts his life in such a way that his happiness is his first priority. He spends half the year in Goa making money through massage and spends the rest of his time travelling around Europe and Asia. He sold his big house in London to finance his lifestyle, and is seemingly unattached to possessions or people, choosing to live with the freedom of coming and going as he pleases. He seems at genuine peace with himself and happy in his rather handsome and youthful skin, which belies his 50 years on earth. In some ways, I felt that David and others like him had paved the way for a lifestyle that appealed to the way I wanted to be. He seemed to appear out of the blue everywhere I went, and as I watched him from the outside, I started to ask myself what was so important about this guy. Was it his free spirit? His lifestyle? His energy? I couldn't quite put my finger on it, but a seed had been planted, and I knew he was sent to teach me and that we would remain friends. And the morning before we were due to leave India, I had a moment of pure knowing, as that seed started to germinate, and my heart opened to a new possibility that I could never have foreseen. I sat the children down, looked them square in the eyes and burst out crying as I told them I wanted to live in Goa. Something deep inside was calling me to stay. This feeling came from my inner self, not my thinking mind but from a deep sense of love inside my heart, which ached for India to be home. It was such a powerful feeling that I could not deny the guidance -it was like destiny calling. That's when I remembered the signs I received all throughout December, when the Diddy song *Coming Home* played constantly in my head every morning and night. I'd shut my eyes and listen to the words. I couldn't escape that song, it was my soul singing to me because she knew she belonged to India. So, in that moment, I made the biggest decision of my life: to move to Goa. It was time to let life, love and God bring me what I needed. I opened my arms and embraced without question the guidance that said this was the path for me. The 46-year-old woman had nothing to do with it. I let go of control. And as I sat there cuddling the children with my newfound sense of freedom, I caught a glimpse of David swimming across the ocean, looking so graceful as he glided through the waves. When it was time to leave Goa and head home to England, I remember collapsing on the floor of Mumbai Airport sobbing my heart out just as I had 25 years earlier as I looked up to Jennifer and said, "I don't want to leave, this is my home."

And she comforted me as she always did and said knowingly, "You'll be back, darling, if anyone can make it happen, you can, Dee, you'll be back."

It was with a heavy heart that I arrived back in England and walked through my front door, feeling the sorrow and pain of the past all over again. I no longer wanted to be in my beautiful home. England became my holding space as I made plans to return to India and start my new life. Within three days I had sealed the deal. I booked our return for 22nd March 2016 – exactly one year on from the most transformational year of my life.

Chapter 17

Living Beyond Limitation

"As human beings, our greatness lies not so much in being able to remake the world – that is the myth of the atomic age – as in being able to remake ourselves" - Ghandi

L earning to keep on moving was the realm of the seventh and final chakra on my journey to healing the self. The crown chakra is called Sahasrara, which means thousandfold, and its purpose is to help expand and grow consciousness beyond the limitations of identifying with the individual self and to a place of universal identity. This is the ultimate purpose of our spiritual practice, where we see from the eyes of oneness and realise finally that everything is connected. And to get to this place we have to let go of attachment and follow the path of wisdom, meditation and morality. For me, attachment was just another word for control. When we control, we are not trusting the wisdom of the universe to give us what we need, we are actually pushing against our suffering rather than seeing it as our greatest teacher. And I fully appreciate that for anyone who has suffered this lesson it is a tough one to get a handle of.

"When we are sure we know something, we run the risk of closing down the crown chakra. New information requires us to expand our belief system, and the refusal to do so closes our system."[32]

My seventh chakra was out of balance because I had got to a place where I was fixated on knowing all the answers to life. I started to develop a new level of certainty that stopped me from being in the flow and put me right back to square one, as I tried to manipulate and control life again. I was convinced I had all the answers and I needed the assurance of being able to predict the future. 'Knowing' was my new buzzword, "but my inner voice quietly whispered, "No, you don't, Dee, you don't know, nobody knows. "And she was right because whenever I thought life was taking me in one direction, I usually ended up going in the other. Life had a plan for me that was far greater than I could ever imagine – and there really is no second-guessing it. The only way to find inner peace was to stop trying to control and manipulate my life, and to start letting it flow through me, allowing the plan to reveal itself minute by minute. I was going round in circles. I knew all this intellectually but living and being in the flow was not always easy, and I didn't always get it right.

And so, I entered the realm of the seventh chakra with a lot of confusion about what to trust. I had evolved through my own suffering to get to a place where I was consciously listening to my inner voice, and I felt like I could trust my intuition. My heart had opened and I started to feel my feelings and use them to guide my decision-making process. But I still needed to see beyond my own limitations, which if I'm honest kept me attached to my desires. The hopeless romantic in me was still looking for its happy ever after, and much of my spiritual development was done in the name of finding a romantic partner. It seems almost juvenile to admit that now, but it's the truth. It was done for my better good and not the good of mankind. It was done to heal the wounds of the mother/child bond and not the bond of Mother Nature. And it was calculated. I travelled this path because I wanted to heal myself. And the seventh chakra healing is beyond all of that. It takes you to a place of being where wants and desires are removed from the equation. It is only when we surrender everything that has kept us bound to a way of being that we truly benefit from the limitless abundance of being.

What does 'being' mean? It means letting go of the need to be right in favour of listening to others' opinions and finding the lessons in what they are telling you. It means examining our belief systems and questioning them. When we say things such as, "I am an artist and artists never make any real money," we are binding ourselves to this belief system and making it our truth. But the fact is it's not true. Personally, I have been stuck in a belief system that told me I wasn't good enough and that I was somehow damaged by my story. These are my beliefs and mine alone. I bind myself to them. Nobody else has that power over me. Nobody. Stepping into the realm of the crown chakra is about stepping into the highest version of self and the archetype of the witness, which is why meditation is so vital in developing the seventh chakra. When we witness life, we allow ourselves to receive information, and when we receive information we are receiving our blessing and stepping into our God-given right to heal and find wholeness.

One of the books that has helped me step into the world of seventh chakra healing is *The Four Agreements* by Don Miguel Ruiz. The book shares four basic agreements to living a life of wisdom. These are:

Be impeccable with your word.
Don't take anything personally.
Don't make assumptions.
Always do your best.

Be impeccable with your word means you really need to think before opening your mouth, which for me is a practice of containment because I have so much to say and I'm not afraid to say it! I would actually benefit by remaining silent more often, allowing others to have a voice. But it also means be mindful of the words you use, the words that say,

"I can't" or "I'm not there yet" or "if only I had more money" or "he's just not my type". Because all these words put limitations around us, and bind us to a negative belief system that blocks us from accessing the abundance of universal love that is available to all.

Don't take anything personally means taking responsibility for all the things you are responsible for. Your words belong to you and not to anybody else. The same applies when you are on the receiving end of words or actions that are hurtful or unpleasant. Those words cannot hurt you, they only hurt the voice that feeds them. So, if your children are screaming at you, don't take it personally – that's their inner voice saying, "I'm hurting." Give them a big hug instead and watch their suffering melt away. That's not to say we invite bad behaviour into our life. We don't. But we know how to guard ourselves against it through nonattachment.

Don't make assumptions is about those times when we get ourselves into a right pickle by misinterpreting a situation. It's OK. We all do it. There is no second-guessing in life. If we want to live authentically, we need to judge each moment on how we feel in that moment, rather than having preconceived ideas and judgements about how things are.

Always do your best means that when you are trying as much as you can you are standing up for yourself and saying, "I'm good enough." You are accepting yourself just as you are in that moment. When you do your best, you step outside your limitations because there are no limitations if what you have done is your best. And when you do your best, you give yourself permission to make mistakes and learn from them. Doing your best is not an excuse to stand back and be complacent, because that wouldn't be doing your best. It means giving yourself permission to love yourself moment by moment because you approve of yourself for doing your best.

Once we awaken as a being of consciousness, our whole experience of our story and the world as we see it awakens and we start to experience our life in a very different way. This is how we get to change the story of the past and heal the wounds that continue to hurt us in the present. We start to bring this conscious stream of awareness back down through the chakra system. At the brow chakra, we start to shine light on the story and see the bigger picture, not just our part in it. At the throat chakra, we start to bring inspired thought into our creativity rather than struggling to find its voice. The voice of creativity now has clarity and purpose. At the heart chakra, we see beyond our own needs and struggles in our relationships with ourselves and others and start to develop compassion. As we work through our own issues, we look on as the relationships around us improve as a result of the wisdom and compassion we are now showing ourselves. At the solar plexus chakra, we turn forced action into transformative action as we energise our intents with vision, wisdom and communication. At the sacral chakra, we make connections with others at a deeper soul level, and we experience love and sexuality with a passion and purity for life itself. And finally, at the root chakra, we bring all the virtues of compassion, wisdom, light and inspiration into our physical reality as we create a world and a life worth living. And we come full circle.

A year after I started on this journey, on 22nd March 2016, I stepped on a plane to India to start a new life with Fionn. This was a life I could never have imagined had I not stopped pushing against mySelf and started to listen to the quiet voice within.

My little boy was welcomed into a new school called The River House Academy on the banks of the Talpona River in South Goa. The school was set up by an inspirational group of women who live and work in Goa and wanted to provide a learning environment which inspires children to become confident, passionate and active global citizens. I knew it was the right place for Fionn the minute I stepped foot through the door. As Fionn settled into school, I searched for somewhere for us to live. I found the perfect place – a 3-bedroom villa with air-conditioning and

Wi-Fi. Everybody told me I'd never find anything like that in Agonda but I did find it, or rather it found me. Like every other magical moment that has happened to me since I stepped foot in Goa, they all seemed to find me at exactly the right time, when I needed them most. This is how *being* showed itself to me. I haven't had to search for anything – everything I have needed or wanted has come to me. It has been truly remarkable.

I also met up with David again, who appeared out of nowhere, as he always did, while I was mooching along the road one day. He was preparing to leave for Europe after a long season in India and was planning to hit the festival scene and live on the road as he partied the summer away and allowed life to take him along in its flow. He was as soft, sensitive and connected as ever, and his friendship was such a gift as he ultimately showed me that I could live another way. David was like a catalyst to me. He taught me a new way of being where there is no should haves, could haves and would haves. He truly lives moment-to-moment, accepting what life gives him. His seemingly ideal lifestyle was worlds apart from mine, but he taught me that freedom is not about a lifestyle. Freedom is about moment-to-moment living wherever we are in the world. I still had a lot of work to do to find the grace within myself to lead such a consciously simple life, but I was headed in the right direction. And if truth be known, David gave me hope, as I could see myself with someone like him, maybe one day.

The season in South Goa comes to an end by the middle of May, as the temperatures rise and the rains come in. Most Westerners return to their homeland for the long, hot monsoon months, as restaurants and shops close down and the beaches and villages are returned to the locals. I returned to the UK for the summer, but the UK was not where I wanted to be. My beautiful house in St Albans ¬– the house that was the little girl's dream – no longer felt like home. I was consciously aware of this feeling of being suspended in time. It was as if the four walls of the house held all the pain and suffering of my past, and I could feel myself being sucked back into the story and the life that I so desperately wanted to leave behind. My soul had moved on and although I tried to enjoy those summer months as best as I could, the truth was I couldn't wait until September to be back on Indian soil again. I was willing my life away and counting down the days until our return. But, in another cruel twist of fate, life stopped me in my tracks and pulled me right back into the story I so desperately wanted to leave behind.

On 10th August 2016, at 7.30 am, I received a phone call from my friend, Emma. I listened to her sob her heart out in stunned silence as she told me the tragic news that her husband Ray Theobald – Tony's best friend – had died instantly of heart failure the night before. I could not believe what I was hearing. In the midst of her suffering, she said to me, "Dee, you're the only person in the world who understands. My whole world has just ended." And this I did know. I knew all too well as the wounds of grief cast their spell on me once again and I mourned the loss of our beautiful Great Raymondo, as we used to call him.

Ray and Tony were inseparable best friends and were like an old married couple. They initially met at work, but their work friendship blossomed into a brotherhood. They called each other every day and spent weekends and holidays together indulging their passion for golf. Ray was also an unmistakable giant of a man who battled with his weight. In his prime, he topped the scales at around 32 stone. There was no hiding when you were in his company. People were drawn to his size but also to his larger-than-life character. And my children loved their great big bear that was uncle Raymondo.

When Tony died, Ray was absolutely heartbroken, and he set about making big changes in his life to get healthy in honour of his best friend. He lost half his body weight and went to the gym every day. To the outside world, he looked like he had regained his fitness and his chance for a healthy life. He also found love in his beautiful wife Emma and the scene was set for their happy ever after when they married in

February 2015. And just like it had with Tony, his life ended in the blink of an eye and without warning. Yet again the close group of old friends were united once more in our shared grief for a life lost too young. This was a hard one to make sense of. And I cried for days. It hurt deeply, and again I felt the wounds of loss and love were as much for Tony as they were for Ray, as I was once again challenged to accept life as it was.

As I walked through pain and surrendered to the tears, I felt like my heart had shattered all over again. But about a week later, Tony's brother called me and said, "Dee, I have something to tell you. We were walking along the marina the day after Ray died and Mum spotted two yachts that were moored up for the day. One was called the Lady Dee and the other one was called the Lady Emma. What are the chances of that? Well, I've come to a place in my life where I believe there are no chances. There are no coincidences. I can no longer accept that life is just a sequence of random events, and I sensed the universe was trying to tell me something. As I closed my eyes and listened to my heart, the message I received was very clear. I was being told that those two friends were reunited again in death. Whatever their connection was through their earthly lives, there was no denying that they were joined again together in spirit. Tony and Ray were still here, and I was being called to share this message with the world.

We said goodbye to the great Raymondo on 6th September 2016, and the next day Fionn and I left the UK and flew back to Goa. And of course, India had plans for us straight away. We didn't move to the dream house in Agonda, as I had intended. Instead, we were guided to an area called Patnem, which was much closer to Fionn's school and closer to the community of mums who welcomed us in with open arms and helped us make the transitions to our new life so much easier. It was the right place to be. Fionn settled back into his Indian school and I went about transforming our two-bedroom apartment into a beautiful home for us both. As I did, I took time out to reflect on the past year and all the amazing lessons that life had brought to me. I felt strength in myself and in the undeniable connection to the world around me. As the light within me started to flicker, this divine feminine energy invited me to a place deep inside, where I started to experience the wholeness of what it means to be a woman. I encountered the goddess in her many manifestations, and I also experienced her darker side and her shadow. And, as I started to grow, I could see how my story resonated with others, as the themes that played out in my life also played out in the collective consciousness of other women. I knew that by telling my story, I could help other women, with their own loss, betrayal and awakening and I felt very humbled by this awareness. As I grew stronger and started to heal, so did many of the people around me. We were doing this together. The year 2016 became an irrefutable year of connectedness and transformation, not just for me, but for all the women around me, who made life-changing moves that set them on a path to a new way of being.

It seemed we are all destined to move on.

My friend, Alex, and her family moved to Ibiza to be close to the nurturing energy of the island. Jennifer moved to Brighton, where she is developing her skills as a heart healing intuitive oracle card reader. Taran, my beautiful yoga teacher and friend, moved back to her home town and set up Holy Cow studio, the first in the area. Of course, there were times when we were frightened, or questioned what the hell we were doing, but in those moments of doubt, one of us was always on the end of the phone to support the other and offer encouragement. As we called upon the sacred feminine energy to rise, it gave us the power to be greater than we ever could have imagined. And as we healed the wounds of our pasts and incorporated this wisdom into our everyday lives, we learnt to receive the wisdom of the generations of women before us. We began to see the archetypal female energy of the lover, the healer, the priestess and the crone in ourselves and in each other, and we drew upon this power, love and wisdom to reinvent ourselves.

We started to feel and experience the true oneness of life, through the consciousness that holds us in its heart.

After I had completed decorating my new apartment, I set about finishing this book. I knew it would be another piece in the jigsaw to opening my heart and letting all the pain of the past go. The book had been holding on as much as I had, and I wanted it to fly so I could get on with my life. But the path to healing is not a quick fix. I'm still a student finding her way, and as I settled into my life in Goa, I realised that my healing had only just begun and there was way more to come. India was healing and revealing parts of me that I never knew existed. And it turned out there was more than just one book that needed to fly. Letting Tony go was one thing, but healing the wounds of my past had become a bit of a masterpiece. Suddenly I realised that I was writing three books, as part of a body of work, which I have called *The Truth is Within*.

The books help people align to their own power which is within. This internal power is sometimes known as Christ Consciousness, but it has nothing to do with religion or even new age spirituality, rather it is an alignment to the goodness, that is within our hearts. When we align to this source within, we light up the path for our own way home, back to our true nature which is love. The first step on this journey is to bring the main chakras back into balance, and I have described how to do this in this book. Once the Chakras are aligned and balanced, the path is clear for life force energy to move freely up and down the central column of our body. This life force connects us to Mother Earth Source energy which nourishes us, and Cosmic Heavenly Energy which activates our higher powers. This connection activates our bodies own innate self-healing powers and we start to transform and heal organically using our own source connection. When we connect to this source of creation, within us, we start to see the world through the eyes of love, whereby we truly understand the inter connectivity of all things, because we experience this connection in everyday life. We start to realise that life is constantly trying to bring us back to our hearts as we commune with nature, and with other people. And when we start to see the world from this elevated position through the higher heart, the wisdom of the heart radically transforms us from the inside out. This wisdom starts to weave itself into our lives and the more we delve into our hearts and trust what comes, the most beautiful, synchronistic events seem to appear out of nowhere. This is how my second book, which is called *Dying and the Art of Being*, came into existence: it just sort of wrote itself. In this book, I explore what it means to die, as I go through my own death process, and experience the true meaning of transcending from one reality to another, which is a stage we all go through once our Consciousness is activated inside. I found that death itself is not the end, rather, it is the beginning of something new. However, it is our fear of death that keeps us stuck in a loop of our own suffering and prevents us from moving forward in life. When we are healing our various behaviours and patterns, we go through many deaths of sorts, where we have to completely let go of our old way of being, to come out the other side. These experiences are never easy and can be extremely hard on us at the time, but they teach us so much about life, because in the end, *it is the love we find for ourselves that actually heals us, and brings us back to our true nature.* This love breathes new life into us, and gives us a life that we simply could never imagine before. And love is a feeling. Love is not something that can be intellectualised, analysed, or understood by reading a book or by going to a Guru or healer. Love has to be integrated, felt and experienced inside of you. You are the only person on earth who can do that for yourself. My third book in the series is called *Within the Heart of Love*, goes on to explore the potency and power of love, as an alchemical tool to transform and change us, through the sacred union, of the masculine and feminine within and without. This book looks at the timeless teachings, myths, and wisdoms that we are being invited to remember at this time of great change on earth. I share some of the deeper mysteries of life, as my

Christ Source Consciousness becomes activated within and without. As I travel around India and France in search of the true meaning of the Holy Grail, I discover the Holy Grail is not outside of me, but the grail is buried deep within my heart.

And so, the journey continues....

Afterword

❖

Before I close this part of the story, I would like to leave you with a few final words.

Never forget that You Are The Way

The wisdom that is self-generated from your own source connection is what ultimately guides you back home to the heart . We live in a world of expectations, where we empower people and things outside ourselves, to be the source of love, that we so desire to feel. This is just the way it is, there is no one to blame, because we are actually only ever accountable to ourselves for our own happiness. And the truth is, most people are trying their best to make sense of this life, especially during times of chaos, when the world is changing radically, and everything we ever believed in has and will be called into question. When we realise nothing outside ourselves will ever fill the void that we feel inside our hearts, we start to turn inwards, and when we do, we begin to heal and transform.

The Truth is Within

As you turn inwards, you start to connect to your own source of love that will never ever fail you. It takes time to really trust ourselves, and the journey inwards has many twists and turns . It's normal to turn to other people for advice, guidance, wisdom, and direction. The seeds of advice that come from others often set us off on a path that isn't necessarily divinely driven, and can take us down many rabbit holes.

This happens to the best of us, and the thing to do when we realise we've taken a wrong turn, is to forgive our self, reclaim our power, and take our own next step forward. Nothing is ever wasted in this journey of life, if we take the time to learn from our mistakes and make things our own.

Live your life authentically

Sometimes when we're on a path of self-discovery we can feel like we have to be a certain way, but it's just not true. This longing to fit in and belong takes us out of our own uniqueness, and can dilute us into something that we are not. Our authenticity is where our true power lies. It's what allows us to shine and grow into a greater version of ourselves. So please honour where you are on your journey inwards, and be kind and compassionate towards yourself when you make mistakes. You are meant to make mistakes, it's how you learn. Don't compare yourself to others or get drawn into their games, it never serves you in the long run. If something resonates you will know to follow that calling because you will feel it in your heart. If something doesn't work for you, you will also know . One day the distinction between what is right and wrong for you will be very clear.

Your words are powerful

You do quite literally write your own story with all that you think, say and do. As you grow and evolve you will start to experience the power of your words play out in your world in real time. This can be fascinating, but also scary, if your heart and mind are not working together as one. But as you start to experience life with this new level of awareness, you begin to take more responsibility for yourself. You learn to master the mind so that it no longer creates chaos in the world. Only then will you become the change you want to see in your world.

Be good, Do good, Keep the faith, Have fun

At the end of the day, life is for living. Sure you want to be your best and strive to leave the world a better place than when you entered, but sometimes we can take ourselves too seriously, and miss out on having fun. So take the time to do the things that bring you joy and happiness, and make you laugh. Laughter is like your heart smiling, it lightens every burden and brings you back into your childlike presence from whence you came.

References

[1] Kenyon, Tom, and Judi Sion. 2002. *The Magdalen Manuscript: The Alchemises of Horus & the Sex Magic of Isis.* London, UK: ORB Communications.

[2] Saraswati, S. C. 2006. *Drops of Nectar: Timeless Wisdom for Everyday Living.* New Delhi: Wisdom Tree.

[3] Saraswati, S. C. 2006. *Drops of Nectar: Timeless Wisdom for Everyday Living.* New Delhi: Wisdom Tree.

[4] Saraswati, S. C. 2006. *Drops of Nectar: Timeless Wisdom for Everyday Living.* New Delhi: Wisdom Tree.

[5] Saraswati, S. C. 2006. *Drops of Nectar: Timeless Wisdom for Everyday Living.* New Delhi: Wisdom Tree.

[6] Lewis, C. S. 1989. *A Grief Observed.* London, UK: Harper Collins.

[7] Saraswati, S. C. 2006. *Drops of Nectar: Timeless Wisdom for Everyday Living.* New Delhi: Wisdom Tree.

[8] Judith, Anodea. 1996. *Eastern Body, Western Mind: Psychology and the Chakra System as a Path to the Self.* Berkeley, CA: Celestial Arts.

[9] Judith, Anodea. 1996. *Eastern Body, Western Mind: Psychology and the Chakra System as a Path to the Self.* Berkeley, CA: Celestial Arts.

[10] I've chosen not to name him to protect his identity.

[11] Judith, Anodea. 1996. *Eastern Body, Western Mind: Psychology and the Chakra System as a Path to the Self.* Berkeley, CA: Celestial Arts.

[12] Norwood, Robin. 2008. *Women Who Love Too Much.* New York City, NY: Pocket Books.

[13] Norwood, Robin. 2008. *Women Who Love Too Much.* New York: Pocket Books.

[14] Storr, Anthony and C. G. Jung. 1983. *The Essential Jung: Selected Writings Introduced by Anthony Storr.* Princeton, NJ: Princeton University Press.

[15] Rogers, C. R. 1967. *On Becoming A Person: A therapist's view of psychotherapy.* London, UK: Constable.

[16] Scaravelli, Vanda. 1991. *Awakening the Spine: The Stress-Free New Yoga that Works with the Body to Restore Health, Vitality and Energy.* London, UK: Harper Collins.

[17] Judith, Anodea. 1996. *Eastern Body, Western Mind: Psychology and the Chakra System as a Path to the Self.* Berkeley, CA: Celestial Arts.

[18] Storr, Anthony and C. G. Jung. 1983. *The Essential Jung: Selected Writings Introduced* by Anthony Storr. Princeton, NJ: Princeton University Press.

[19] Waheed, Nayyirah. 2013. *salt.* Charleston: Createspace.

[20] Waheed, Nayyirah. 2013. *salt.* Charleston: Createspace.

[21] Steiner, Rudolph, and Michael Wilson. 1964. *The Philosophy of Freedom.* Forest Row, UK: Rudolf Steiner.

[22] Peck, M, S. 2006. *The Road Less Travelled.* London, UK: Arrow.

[23] Storr, Anthony and C. G. Jung. 1983. *The Essential Jung: Selected Writings Introduced* by Anthony Storr. Princeton, NJ: Princeton University Press.

[24] Judith, Anodea. 1996. *Eastern Body, Western Mind: Psychology and the Chakra System as a Path to the Self.* Berkeley, CA: Celestial Arts.

[25] Judith, Anodea. 1996. *Eastern Body, Western Mind: Psychology and the Chakra System as a Path to the Self.* Berkeley, CA: Celestial Arts.

[26] Waheed, Nayyirah. 2013. *salt.* Charleston: Createspace.

[27] Siegal, D. J. and Mary Hartzell. 2014 *Parenting from the Inside Out: How a deeper self-understanding can help you raise children who thrive.* Victoria, Australia: Scribe.

[28] Judith, Anodea. 1996. *Eastern Body, Western Mind: Psychology and the Chakra System as a Path to the Self.* Berkeley, CA: Celestial Arts.

[29] Judith, Anodea. 1996. *Eastern Body, Western Mind: Psychology and the Chakra System as a Path to the Self.* Berkeley, CA: Celestial Arts.

[30] Judith, Anodea. 1996. *Eastern Body, Western Mind: Psychology and the Chakra System as a Path to the Self.* Berkeley, CA: Celestial Arts.

[31] Hawkins, David. 1995. *Power vs Force: The Hidden Determination of Human Behaviour.* Sedona, Az: Veritas.

[32] Judith, Anodea. 1996. *Eastern Body, Western Mind: Psychology and the Chakra System as a Path to the Self.* Berkeley, CA: Celestial Arts.

Acknowledgements

I would like to express my heartfelt gratitude to all the people who have loved and supported me over the years.

To my children Millie and Fionn for being bright lights in my world.

To my Mother and Father who taught me resilience and what it means to be family.

To my brothers and sisters. For allowing me to be the 'good' one in the gang. I hope I played my role well.

To Tony, Martyn and Paul. The men in my life who loved and helped me become the woman I am today.

To my Besties, Debbie, Natalie, Sharon, Angela, Anna, Laura and Vanessa. For always being there, You are my rocks.

To my Soulsisters Alex, Jennifer, and Taran for all the crazy woo woo conversations, and moon rituals. The Magic works.

To Danielle Wrate for being the first person to pick up my story and for helping me bring it to life. Thank you for believing in me.

To Rev. Ariel Patricia for reminding me that it is my own story that really counts.

To Patricia Frida, who created the new artwork for the re-edits. They are divine.

To Greg Scott, for his badass editing skills. And for being a mentor to my son.

To all the spiritual warriors, too many to mention, living their best lives and helping humanity along the way. Together we've got this.

About the Author

Dee Delaney was born in the UK to Irish parents and lived in India and Southeast Asia for over 10 years. She developed a profound love for the East from an early age, and she is extremely sensitive to the injustices in the world, especially when it comes to disadvantaged women and children. Dee had worked at the BBC for many years when her husband, Tony, died suddenly while doing a charity mountain climb. His death, along with the subsequent deaths of two former partners, her father and a best friend changed her perspective on life, and in 2016, she embarked on a seven-year spiritual quest, swapping her charmed life in the West for a simpler existence in Goa and then Bali. As a result of this journey of self-discovery, she wrote a trilogy of books called *The Truth is Within*, and her writing is ingrained with the insights she gained during her spiritual odyssey. Dee has now returned to the UK to be close to friends and family, and when she's not travelling, she works as a spiritual coach helping others to connect to their divinity within.

To discover more visit www.deedelaney.co.uk or join her community on Facebook and Instagram @deedelaney01

By the Same Author

Dying and the Art of Being
(Book 2 in *The Truth is Within* trilogy)
Navigating Our Fears Around Death, Dying and Endings of all Kind

Dee takes her story to a sleepy fishing village in South Goa, India, where she builds a new life for herself and her young son. But the brutal murder of a young Irish girl stops Dee in her tracks, calling her into the pain, suffering and injustices of the world, which triggers a deep remembrance inside.

In the second book of her trilogy, Dee invites the reader to explore the nature of reality through the death and dying process. She shares rare insights and wisdom from Tibetan Buddhism, alongside practical tips from her training with the Soul Midwives, who use ancient practices to assist those who are dying. As she wrote Book 2, she worked with a sacred oil called spikenard, which helped to expand her consciousness in preparation for her own near-death experience in Bali.

Within the Heart of Love
(Book 3 in *The Truth is Within* trilogy)
Liberating the Mind and Expanding Consciousness

Dee's story moves from India to Bali, where she lived during the Covid pandemic, and where a remarkable near-death experience frees her mind and changes her entire outlook on the world once again. As her life is transformed, Dee revisits events from her past, exploring themes such as healing, sexuality, religion, relationships, and our connection with the universe and each other.

In the final part of her trilogy, Dee explains the awakening process through myths, stories, poetry and ancient wisdom, which she accessed through past lives. Her book is designed to energetically activate the heart, and Dee describes the three stages to self-realisation, inviting the reader to explore their own selves through a template called "10 Ways to Live in Divine Union," which can be used to help navigate these challenging times.